SOLO COOKING
FOR A SUSTAINABLE PLANET

by JOYCE LEBRA

ISBN: 978-1-48356-949-9

CONTENTS

INTRODUCTION

I   SOUPS

II   SALADS

III   SAUCES, DIPS, AND DRESSINGS

IV   LEGUMES

V   OTHER VEGETABLES

VI   FISH

VII   RICE AND OTHER GRAINS

VIII   EGGS, CHEESE, TOFU, NUTS, SEEDS

IX   BREADS AND MUFFINS

X   DESSERTS

APPENDICES

        Useful Items for the Larder

INTRODUCTION

There are many cogent reasons in today's environment for becoming a vegetarian, pescetarian, or following a Mediterranean diet. The effects of chemicals, greenhouse gasses and other pollutants are cumulative and therefore impossible to ignore. Corals are dying in the oceans and species are going extinct everywhere. Extinction is forever, not reversible. Genetic modification of plants and animals destroys natural strains of seeds and affects animals is some ways as yet unknown. Films such as Al Gore's have clearly delineated the nature of the environmental crisis.

Over half our agricultural land is devoted to feeding animals with genetically modified crops, not their natural grass diet. Moreover, hormones and antibiotics fed to cattle, hogs and chickens often foster drug-resistant diseases.

All these factors add up to an unsustainable pattern of animal and human eating habits. Moreover, three and a half ounces of fish contain the same amount of protein as three and a half ounces of chicken and beef.

This book therefore advocates a vegetarian/pescetarian diet approximating a Mediterranean or traditional Japanese diet.

These concerns also do not even address spiritual or ethical considerations which deter many vegetarians from eating meat. Seeing chickens force-fed or calves cooped up in cramped pens and fed grains is not conducive to consuming these animals. Arguments also abound for eating organic rather than genetically altered grains and vegetables, since those crops have increasing amounts of chemical additives and are increasingly taking over agricultural land. The over-consumption of meat and dairy products by Americans has also contributed to the: a highest incidence of diabetes, heart disease, cancer, and obesity of any industrial nation. Japanese people who follow a traditional diet have a much lower incidence of these diseases and have one of the longest life spans in the world. The somewhat similar Mediterranean diet relying heavily on the consumption of fruits and vegetables and the use of grains and olive oil is equally beneficial.

There is one caveat about eating fish, however. The oceans have also become polluted, in some areas worse than others. Over-fishing has depleted formerly rich fishing grounds. Eating fish is subject to some risks, since large fish such as tuna contain a high proportion of mercury. Using a guide such as the Monterey Bay Fish Guide points us to the best and worst choices.

I have lived and worked in Japan for a total of ten years and in India for over three and a half years, and my diet has evolved partly under the influence of the cuisines of those two countries. This book accordingly reflects those tastes. I have also spent many months working in Southeast Asia and I enjoy Thai cuisine as well as some Chinese methods of cooking. I have become a pescetarian, which basically follows a Mediterranean or traditional Japanese diet, based on fish, soy products, grains, fruits and vegetables and generally eschews beef and pork.

Because I have also lived alone for most of my life, I have developed cooking strategies for preparing small portions or a habit of preparing meals for more than one day and freezing portions for later consumption.

A strong reason for turning my attention to these concerns is also the fact that I hear many single friends say, "I live alone so I don't cook," or worse, "I don't care what I put in my stomach." The assumption behind these statements appears to be that it is not worth preparing a delicious meal for a single person. I have heard similar statements so often that I decided I needed to do something to try to alter this mind set. This is another reason I have written this book.

Cooking can be and is for me a creative, challenging, and relaxing activity. Any recipe can be a subject for a novel and delicious experiment, and the result is so delectable! Theoretically it is possible to assemble any combination of ingredients, the only limitations being one's imagination or taste preferences. I sincerely hope that this book will inspire people, whether single or otherwise, to take a bit more care in the kitchen, to experiment. The most delectable dishes are not always the ones that require the most preparation time. Since my approach is to encourage experimentation, I do not always specify exact amounts except in the case of baking. I also encourage readers to try alternate combinations of ingredients.

Beyond healthy dietary habits, what can the individual do about this environmental crisis? Of course supporting political initiatives by elected representatives in an option, though the results are often frustrating. We can also support one or more of the many organizations devoted to protecting the environment: the Sierra Club, the Nature Conservancy, Ocean Conservancy, the World Wildlife Fund, and others.

As individuals we may grow our own fruits and vegetables, whether in an outdoor garden or patio or in pots on a balcony. To garden effectively we need to enhance the soil with organic mulch and ensure adequate sun and water. Artificial pesticides and herbicides kill bees which are necessary for pollination. A natural spray of a tincture of mint and garlic is effective.

A large factor in sustainability of the economy is consuming locally grown produce. Transporting food across continents and oceans is wasteful and not cost-effective or sustainable in the long run. Moreover, shipping food for long distances means that fruit and vegetables must be picked before they are ripe, and the resulting food is not as tasteful as locally grown produce.

In addition to all these problems, the population of the planet has reached a level where the food and water supply is inadequate, unsustainable. Population planning is obviously imperative. A wide range of options is thus available to us as consumers concerned with sustainability.

The goal of this book is to encourage reluctant or very busy individuals to venture into the kitchen for more than a glass of water or piece of toast.

This book is organized according to main ingredients, from soup to dessert. Bon Appetit, as Julia always said!

[I]

SOUPS

Soup making is one of the most ancient and also versatile of cuisines. Probably soon after fire was discovered women began to combine ingredients in large crocks or vessels of clay over a fire. It is a satisfying and can be creative way to cook and produces marvelous gustatory pleasures. Recipes are included here in this conviction, with the hope that each cook will be encouraged to experiment and to discover the joy of making and eating soup.

All soups are made from a basic stock, in this case a stock based on vegetables or fish. Vegetable stock powder is available in many stores, or it can be made starting with fish, mushrooms, or a combination of vegetables. Stocks can be stored in the freezer for later use, a handy strategy for solo cooks. Soups can be clear or cream/potage. For thickening I prefer a potato puree to a flour roux. Herbs and spices are often the key to a truly distinctive soup, and a great variety is available. I like to experiment and hope readers will also. Soups are a gratifying comfort in cold weather, but some cold soups for hot weather are also included here.

Ingredients I keep in my larder for soup making include stock, onions, scallions and/or leeks, celery, garlic, carrots, potatoes, tomato sauce, /tomatoes, herbs such as parsley, cilantro, basil, dill and thyme, and spices including cumin, coriander, cardamom, turmeric, garam masala, and cayenne. I also keep on hand soy sauce, sake, nori, wakame, and bonito flakes for Japanese-inspired recipes.

For solo cooking I find the Smart Stick very useful, as small portions can be efficiently blended or pureed. For lentil and legume soups, since they require longer cooking, I generally make enough for four or more servings at a time. Of course any of the recipes in this book may be expanded when cooking for guests or to freeze a portion for later use. When making soup I generally prepare more than one portion, as day old soup is even better than freshly made.

Black Bean Soup

Soak 1 cup of black beans overnight (or use 1 can). Raw ingredients are preferable to canned beans which contain additives that may not be conducive to good health.

> 5 cups stock or water
>
> 1 onion, chopped (shallot or leek can be substituted)
>
> 1 tablespoon cumin powder or roasted and ground
>
> 1 carrot, chopped
>
> 1 garlic clove
>
> 1 tomato, sliced
>
> ½ cup chopped ripe olives
>
> Parsley
>
> Salt and pepper to taste

Sauté onion and add cumin. Simmer beans in stock for 45 minutes, then add onion, carrot tomato and summer until all are tender. When nearly done, add olives. Garnish with parsley or cilantro. Can be frozen if not consumed when cooked. Solo cooks can use one-third or one-half of this recipe. Since dried beans take quite a while to soak and cook I generally make more than a single serving. This recipe will serve four or five. Since beans require longer cooking than other ingredients, I include larger recipes than for one person.

Acorn Squash Soup

Cut squash in half and seed. Bake or cook in microwave. Save liquid or use stock. This recipe is adequate for half a squash, for a single serving.

1 teaspoon grated ginger

1 teaspoon. onion, chopped

Juice and zest of half an orange

½ teaspoon cumin powder

½ teaspoon nutmeg grated

Pinch of cayenne pepper if desired

Sauté onion till translucent, then add ginger, cumin and nutmeg.

Put cut up cooked squash and other ingredients in a blender and blend.

This can be prepared in any quantity. For a single serving half a small acorn squash is usually enough. Adjust quantities of other ingredients accordingly.

Garnish with parsley or cilantro.

Variation: an amount of greens may be added: spinach, chard, kale, etc. at the last stage of cooking

Root Vegetable Soup for one

Cut up a combination of two or more of the following, totaling about ⅔ cup:

Carrot	1 tablespoon onion, chopped
Parsnip	2 teaspoons oil or butter
Sweet potato	Salt and pepper to taste
Turnip	Choice of herbs

Adjust vegetable amount to whether or not you are preparing the soup for one person or more.

Sauté onion, shallot or leek in oil or butter till translucent. Simmer vegetables in 1-2 cup stock until tender. Blend all in a blender, small food processor or use a "smart stick." Season with salt, pepper and mixed herbs (mixtures can be purchased)

Or use parsley or herbs of preference. I tend toward cilantro often. Cumin is also a good addition to most vegetable soups.

Mushroom Soup for one

1 tablespoon olive oil or butter.

1 tablespoon onions, leeks or scallions, chopped

1 tablespoon chopped red bell pepper

3 medium sized mushrooms, sliced

1 tablespoon flour

½ cup milk, cream or half and half

Sauté onion, red pepper and mushrooms in oil or butter. Add flour gradually and mix, then add milk or cream gradually. To thin, add a small amount of vegetable stock. Season with salt, pepper, paprika. Garnish with parsley.

For oil, a useful combination of olive oil and butter is commercially available.

Cream of Parsnip Soup for one

1 shallot or 1 tablespoon chopped onions or leeks

1 tablespoon oil or butter

1 small parsnip, sliced

2 tablespoons chopped celery

1-2 tablespoons white wine

1 cup stock

¼ teaspoon balsamic vinegar

3 tablespoons half and half

Sauté onion or shallot and celery in butter. Add 2 tablespoons white wine and reducc.

Add sliced parsnip, stock, and balsamic vinegar. Simmer till tender. Puree. Bits of carrot or turnip may be added, chopped, to this soup for a richer flavor. Add half and half and season with salt and pepper.

Asparagus Soup for one

1 tablespoon butter

1 tablespoon onion or leek, chopped

1 cup stock

8-10 stocks asparagus, tough ends cut off

1 small potato, peeled and cubed

Fresh thyme

Sauté onions and leeks, cook asparagus in stock. Cook potato in1 cup stock.

Combine all in blender or use smart stick. Thicken with pureed potato When using onions, shallots and/or leeks for a vegetable soup recipe, be careful that these vegetables do not over-power the main vegetable.

Broccoli Soup for one

1 tablespoon butter or oil

2 tablespoons onion, chopped

1 cup broccoli pieces

1 cup stock

⅓ cup milk or half and half

Salt, pepper to taste

Dash of basil

Lemon zest, about ¼ teaspoon

Parsley, marjoram, tarragon or thyme leaves for garnish.

Sauté onion in oil till translucent. A bit of chopped celery may be added with the onion.

Cook broccoli in stock, reserving some flowerets. Add pepper, thyme, basil and lemon zest and cook till broccoli is tender. Add milk or cream and blend. Add reserved flowerets. Garnish with cheese and chives or coriander leaves.

Variations: sliced apple or green bell pepper can be added during cooking onion, but not so much that it over powers the broccoli flavor.

Zucchini Soup for one

1 cup sliced small zucchini	1 teaspoon curry powder
1 tablespoon oil or butter	¼ teaspoon lemon zest
1 tablespoon chopped onion	½ teaspoon fresh dill
½ teaspoon ginger root, chopped	2 tablespoons milk or table cream
1 teaspoon garlic, chopped	

Sauté onion and garlic in oil a few minutes. Add curry powder and ginger and cook an additional minute. Add zucchini and cook 5 minutes. Remove from heat and add milk or cream and dill. Puree all in blender. Add salt and pepper. Tarragon is also an optional herb for this recipe, but use sparingly.

Variation: This soup can also be served cold, in which case the zucchini need not be cooked prior to blending. Garnish with Parmesan cheese.

Borscht for one

2 tablespoons onions, chopped

1 cup stock   ½ teaspoon salt

4 tablespoons celery, chopped   Dash of pepper

1 medium beet, peeled and chopped or sliced

½ cup cabbage, sliced or grated   2 teaspoons red wine vinegar

1 small potato, sliced   Dill leaves

Sauté onion and celery in oil till translucent, about 8 minutes. Add stock, beets, potato and summer till beets and potato are tender but not mushy, about 35 minutes.

Garnish with a dollop of sour cream or yogurt. A bit of red wine vinegar may be added, about 1 Tablespoon or less. Can be prepared a day ahead and refrigerated, covered. Traditionally, Russian cooks may have used rendered bacon fat, but since this book does not use meat, we have eliminated bacon fat. This recipe may be enough for two servings.

Variation: Puree all ingredients with ¼ cup sour cream or yogurt, or alternatively, add it as a garnish. The Russian version includes cabbage and carrot.

Carrot Ginger Soup for one

1 tablespoon oil or butter

1 medium carrot, sliced or chopped

1 small red potato, sliced

1 tablespoon onion, sliced or chopped

1 cup stock

¼ teaspoon ginger root, chopped

1 teaspoon cumin powder

2 tablespoons cream or half and half

Sauté onion in oil till translucent, then add ginger root and cumin and cook one more minute, then add ginger and cook briefly. Simmer carrot and potato in stock till tender. Combine all, add salt and pepper to taste. Add a pinch of cayenne or red pepper flakes if desired. Add milk or cream and pure in blender.

Cauliflower Soup

1 tablespoon butter or oil

1 ½ tablespoons onion or shallots, chopped

⅔ cup cauliflower pieces and flowerets

1 small potato (⅓ cup, chopped)

1 teaspoon cumin powder or toasted and ground seeds

¼ cup milk, cream or half and half

Salt and pepper to taste

Dash of cayenne

Grated Parmesan cheese to garnish

Sauté onion in oil till translucent, about 5 minutes. Add cumin and vegetables and reduce heat. Add stock and simmer till vegetables are tender, about 25 minutes.

Reserve flowerets. Puree soup mixture in blender. Add salt and pepper, flowerets and milk or cream. Garnish with grated cheese.

Variation: Coriander and/or cardamom may be added also. Or 1 tablespoon lemon juice or white wine may be added when serving. Chopped chives or parsley may be added to garnish.

Potato and Leek Soup

1 tablespoon oil or butter

1 small leek, sliced

1 small potato, peeled and sliced

2 tablespoons chopped celery

1 tablespoon onion, chopped

1 cup stock

¼ teaspoon. grated nutmeg

2 tablespoons cream or half and half

1 tablespoon minced parsley

Salt and pepper to taste

Sauté onion, leek, and celery in oil for about 10 minutes. Add stock and potato, nutmeg and parsley and simmer covered till potato is tender. Blend, then return to saucepan. Add milk or cream and heat. Add lemon zest and garnish with nutmeg and parsley. A bit of dry white wine may be added, about 1 or 2 teaspoons Madeira or sherry is also a nice addition rather than white wine.

Roasted Red Pepper and Tomato Bisque

½ a red bell pepper

1 small tomato

1 tablespoon olive oil

1 tablespoon onion, chopped

½ teaspoon sugar

1 cup stock

½ a bay leaf

1 teaspoon sherry

¼ teaspoon sherry vinegar

salt and pepper to taste

dash of cayenne

Roast bell pepper till blackened. Let it cool, then peel. Heat oil in a saucepan over medium high heat. Sauté onion till translucent. Add tomato, sugar and cook about 5 minutes. Stir in stock, bay leaf, salt and pepper and bring to boil. Simmer a few minutes.

Discard bay leaf and add bell pepper, sherry, vinegar and cayenne. Purée in a blender.

Variations: Try adding mustard seeds, chopped cilantro, or garnish with sour cream and cilantro, marjoram or rosemary.

Sweet Potato Soup with Indian Seasonings

1 tablespoon onion, chopped

2 teaspoons olive oil

1 small sweet potato, peeled and diced

2 tablespoons chopped red bell pepper

½ teaspoon coriander

Salt and pepper to taste

½ teaspoon ground cardamom

1 tablespoon sour cream or yogurt

1 cup stock

Sauté onion in oil till translucent. Add coriander and cook 1 minute. Add stock and sweet potato and simmer till potatoes are tender. Blend and add salt and pepper. In a separate bowl mix sour cream with cardamom and garnish soup with cream mixture.

Minestrone Soup for one

1 small tomato, peeled and quartered

2 tablespoons chopped celery

2 tablespoons sliced carrot

2 tablespoons sliced mushrooms

2 tablespoons dried beans mixture

Salt and pepper to taste

1 teaspoon chopped garlic

½ teaspoon oregano and basil

1 cup stock

Put all in a heavy pan or Dutch oven and simmer one hour. Dried beans take longer than the other ingredients and may be simmered for 30 minutes before adding other ingredients. A bit of bay leaf may also be added during the subsequent 30 minutes of cooking. Parsley and pesto are also often added to this tomato-based soup.

Miso Soup

2 tablespoons or 1 small packet dried bonito flakes

1 ½ cup water

3 tablespoons miso paste

1 tablespoon chopped green onion

A few cubes of tofu

A few pieces of kombu, broken up

A few squares of wakame, cut up

Instant miso soup packages are available. However, for the original miso soup take the bonito flakes and put into 1 ½ cup boiling water. Boil for 10-12 minutes, then drain, reserving the clear soup base. Boil with kombu pieces for 3 or 4 minutes. Add miso paste, either red or white, mix with the hot stock and simmer a few minutes longer, stirring until the miso paste is dissolved. Add a few squares of wakame seaweed for a few minutes, then remove it from the soup. Add chopped green onion and tofu cubes. These ingredients are available from Oriental food stores or health food stores like Vitamin Cottage.

Pinto Bean Soup for one

1 tablespoon onion, shallot or leek, chopped

1 tablespoon oil	1 cup stock
1 tablespoon carrot, chopped	1 teaspoon olives, chopped
1 tablespoon celery, chopped	Dash of oregano & basil
½ teaspoon garlic, chopped	Salt and pepper to taste
¼ cup cooked pinto beans	1 teaspoon red wine
1 teaspoon tomato sauce	

Sauté onion in oil till translucent. Add celery and carrot and cook another 4 minutes. Add garlic, oregano, basil, and pepper. Add tomato sauce and beans to stock and simmer, adding all ingredients together. Simmer for 10 more minutes. Serve with parsley and add salt to taste. I don't add salt until the last stage, if at all, in preparing soups, as many homemade soups are overly salty. Salt can always be added but not subtracted from soup.

Lentil Soup with Cheese

1 tablespoon olive oil

1 tablespoon onion, chopped

1 tablespoon carrot, chopped

1 tablespoons celery, sliced

1 cup stock

¼ cup lentils-red

2 tablespoons crumbled cheese, Stilton or goat

Salt and pepper to taste

2 teaspoons chives, chopped

Sauté onion in oil. Add stock and lentils and bring to boil. Add carrot and celery. Simmer 40 minutes until tender. Garnish with chives and cheese.

Variations: Basil, oregano and thyme may be added instead of cheese. Another option is to omit both cheese and herbs and instead add a bit of cubed parsnip, 2 teaspoons sherry and garnish with yogurt mixed with a dash of grated horseradish. This latter version may be pureed before garnishing.

Split Pea Soup

½ cup split peas	Salt to taste
1 tablespoon onion, chopped	Generous shake of black pepper
½ teaspoon garlic, chopped	Drizzle of sesame oil to serve
1 tablespoon carrot, cubed	Drizzle of red wine vinegar
1 tablespoon potato, cubed	1 tablespoon celery, sliced
1 ½ cup water	

Place peas in water and bring to boil, then simmer partly covered 20 minutes.

Add all vegetables, either sautéed in oil or raw and simmer another 40 minutes, adding water as necessary. Serve with drizzle of sesame oil and red wine vinegar. Garnish with mint, dill and/or parsley. Often a bit of ham is added, if you are carnivorous.

Variation: 2 tablespoons frozen green peas may be added in the final stage, with a generous helping of mint for garnish. Rice, quinoa, or millet may be added for a heartier soup.

Indian Garbanzo Soup (Dhal)

1 tablespoon onion, chopped

1 tablespoon oil

1 tablespoon Anaheim pepper, chopped

1 cherry tomato, halved

1 teaspoon garlic, chopped

1 teaspoon lemon juice

1 ½ cup stock, heated to boiling

⅓ can garbanzos

Ground spices, mixed as follows:

Dash of cumin, coriander, turmeric, cinnamon, cloves, black pepper, salt

Sauté onion and garlic in oil. When light brown, add spice mixture and fry 2-4 minutes. Add stock, garbanzos and simmer. Add lemon juice.

Variation: mushrooms, green peas, and/or chopped greens such as spinach, chard, or kale may be added for color. This is also called dhal in India. It is often made with lentils.

African Peanut & Shrimp Soup

1 tablespoon onion, chopped	1 cup stock
1 tablespoon carrot, chopped	3 tablespoons peanut butter
1 tablespoon celery, chopped	1 or 2 large shrimp
1 tablespoon bell pepper, chopped	Salt, pepper to taste
1 teaspoon garlic, chopped	Cayenne
1 cherry tomato	1 tablespoon oil

Sauté vegetables in oil. Bring stock to a boil, then simmer, with peanut butter, tomato and shrimp. Add sautéed vegetables and simmer 20 minutes. Season with salt, pepper and cayenne to taste.

Variation: 2 tablespoons of chopped greens such as kale or chard, or green peas or garbanzos may be added.

Vichyssoise

½ cup cubed russet potatoes

2 tablespoons leeks, onion or scallion

1 tablespoon butter

1 tablespoon cucumber, sliced

1 cup stock

2 tablespoons half and half or cream

1 teaspoon red wine vinegar

1 tablespoon chopped mint leaves

Pepper and salt to taste

Sauté onion or leek in butter. Peel and cube potatoes. Peel, seed and chop cucumber and add both to onion with stock. Cook until soft and puree. Cool and add half and half, vinegar and mint. Garnish with mint.

Variation: Dill may be substituted for mint. For more traditional vichyssoise omit mint, vinegar and cucumber. Add 1 tablespoon carrot, chopped. Another version uses sorrel rather than mint, omitting vinegar and adding chives.

Salmon Chowder

⅓ - ½ cup canned salmon

1 small shallot

  Or 1 tablespoon leek, chopped

½ celery stalk sliced

1 teaspoon butter or oil

¼ cup potato, peeled, cubed

¼ cup milk or half and half

Dash of dill, parsley leaf, coriander

Salt and pepper to taste

1 cup water

Briefly Sauté shallot and celery in oil. Add all other ingredients except milk and simmer until potatoes are done. Then add milk or cream and heat briefly.

Fish chowder can be made with any white fish such as halibut, sole, tilapia, cod, etc.

Variation: canned corn or frozen peas are a compatible addition to this chowder.

Bouillabaisse for six

½ bottle clam juice

saffron threads

1 bay leaf, 2 tablespoons fennel bulb

fennel leaf, celery leaves, parsley

Bag of frozen fish including mussels, shrimp, scallops

½ pound barramundi or other white fish

1 tomato

2 tablespoons each carrots, onions, sweet red pepper, celery

2 tablespoons olive oil

1 tablespoon white wine

Prepare two stocks: one with clam juice, saffron threads and water as needed during simmering. The second stock is made with bay leaf, fennel bulb and leaf, leek, celery and parsley, simmered with water or vegetable stock. These stocks may be stored overnight in the refrigerator. Sauté all vegetables in oil. When onion is translucent, combine all vegetables, stocks and fish and simmer for 30 or more minutes. The Italian version, cioppino, uses more fish and tomatoes. Since this soup requires more than usual preparation time I generally make a larger batch.

Avocado Cucumber Soup

1 peeled and cut up ripe avocado

1 small peeled, seeded, and sliced cucumber

½ cup stock

1-2 teaspoons lemon juice

¼ cup buttermilk

1 teaspoon cumin

1 teaspoon oil

Heat cumin in oil briefly in frying pan. Combine with all other ingredients in blender and puree. Serve chilled. Garnish with cilantro. This is my favorite summer soup and is very refreshing.

Gazpacho

½ cup tomato juice

1 tablespoon minced onion

1 teaspoon garlic, minced

1 tablespoon cucumber, minced

2 teaspoons olive oil

½ cup diced fresh tomatoes

1 teaspoon red wine vinegar

dash of basil, oregano, cumin

1 tablespoon bell pepper, minced

Salt, pepper, cayenne to taste

1 teaspoon lemon juice

Tomato sauce with basil may be substituted for juice and fresh tomato.

Put all ingredients in blender and puree. Garnish with flat leaf parsley.

Variation: This soup may be served hot, and if you add tortilla chips it becomes tortilla soup. You may prefer not to blend all but to leave some in chunks. A bit of salsa may be added if you like yours spicy.

Minted Green Pea Soup

1 teaspoon olive oil or butter

1 tablespoon chopped sweet onion or scallion

1 cup shelled fresh green peas

1 teaspoon chopped mint

1 teaspoon chopped parsley

1 cup vegetable broth

½ cup buttermilk

Sauté onion in oil. Add peas, mint, parsley and broth. Stir and bring to a boil, then reduce heat and simmer 15 minutes. Then puree in blender of with Smart Stick until smooth. Press soup through a sieve and discard pea fibers. Add buttermilk, salt and pepper to taste. Serve chilled with a mint sprig.

Pumpkin Soup

1 can pumpkin puree	½ - 1 teaspoon red curry paste
⅓ cup coconut milk	½ teaspoon cumin seed
1 ½ tablespoons oil	1 piece fresh ginger root, diced
1 medium onion, chopped	Salt to taste
1 clove garlic, minced	2-3 cups stock

Heat oil in a skillet. Add onion, garlic, cumin seed and cook over medium heat, stirring often, until onion is soft. Add stock and curry paste; cover and simmer gently until onion is tender, about 10-15 minutes. Transfer to a blender or food processor. Add pumpkin, coconut milk and ginger. Puree until smooth. Return to saucepan and cook 5 minutes to blend flavors.

[II]

SALADS

When we think of salads we generally think of lettuce, spinach, arugula, radiccio, endive, and other greens as the main ingredient. Salads, however, can be made from a combination of virtually any vegetables or fruits, fresh, raw, or cooked, and may include a variety of other ingredients such as cheese, eggs, nuts, tofu, fish, or even noodles. They can be easily assembled by solo cooks, either for dining alone or with others. A salad can be the main component of a meal or an accompaniment. In other words, salads are one of the most versatile parts of a meal as well as being healthful and easy to prepare. I generally have a salad every day, either at noon or in the evening. The recipes included here by no means exhaust the possibilities.

I assume that every cook, even the least enthusiastic or experienced, has a favorite recipe for potato salad and also for a three-bean salad, and I therefore do not include these common salads here. I hope to encourage cooks to experiment using ingredients with which they may not be familiar, since it is all too easy to fall into a culinary rut, eating the same thing day after day, week after week. One of the goals of this book is to encourage cooks who may not be experienced to venture beyond the usual, to explore unfamiliar ingredients. If you always have lettuce in your salad, try spinach or arugula instead. The kitchen is your lab, and experimentation is one of the satisfactions, one of the "joys of cooking."

Beet and Egg Salad

1 cooked beet, cubed, or 5 or 6 slices of canned beets

1 egg, hard-boiled and sliced or quartered

½ celery stalk, sliced

1 roma tomato, quartered

1 green onion, sliced

Combine all ingredients and dress.

Dressing:

1 teaspoon olive oil

½ teaspoon red wine vinegar or balsamic vinegar

Salt and pepper to taste

Variation: ½ teaspoon mustard and ½ teaspoon sugar may be added to vinaigrette

Add parsley or cilantro as garnish.

Waldorf Salad

1 cup fresh spinach

Several mandarin orange sections

4 walnuts, cut up

½ an apple, peeled and sliced

Variation: other greens may be substituted for spinach.

Dressing: vinaigrette, in any variation

Walnuts should be roasted in oil, then rolled in sugar for crispness and sweetness.

Red Cabbage Coleslaw

½ a red cabbage, sliced thinly or grated in a processor

½ a red onion, sliced thinly

1 celery stalk, sliced

Marinate cabbage and onion overnight with marinade.

Marinade:

1 tablespoon red wine vinegar

1 tablespoon sugar

1 tablespoon yellow mustard seed

2 tablespoons brown mustard seed

1 tablespoon caraway seed

1 tablespoon black peppercorn in a sachet

Marinate coleslaw overnight.

Spinach and Mushroom Salad

1 cup fresh spinach

1 large mushroom, sliced

1 walnut, chopped, if desired

Walnuts can be sautéed in oil, then rolled in sugar when hot.

 Dressing:

Vinaigrette: add ½ teaspoon honey and ½ teaspoon mustard to vinaigrette.

Balsamic vinegar is best for this salad. This is a simple salad and one of my favorites.

Roasted Red Pepper and Cucumber Salad

6 slices red bell pepper

6 slices cucumber

2 teaspoons olive oil

1 clove garlic, chopped

Roast a red pepper with 2 teaspoons of olive oil and chopped garlic. When peppers have cooled peel, slice, combine with cucumber slices. This is a simple but not very common salad.

Pinto or White Bean Salad

¼ cup cooked beans

1 tablespoon celery, sliced

5 slices cucumber, peeled

1 teaspoon red onion, sliced

Salt and pepper to taste

1 teaspoon olive oil

Dash of basil and dill

1 cherry tomato, halved

1 tablespoon chopped red bell pepper

Combine all ingredients. Dress with vinaigrette of olive oil and balsamic vinegar.

Turkish variation: add some chopped black olives and 1 teaspoon capers, drained, and also a few hot red pepper flakes. Sliced celery may also be added to this salad.

Lime Jello Salad

1 package lime jello

1 cup boiling water, to dissolve jello

1 cup cold water (part pineapple juice may be used)

1 tart apple, peeled and diced

1 small can pineapple, crushed or sliced and cubed

Dressing: generally a light mayonnaise or mayonnaise combined with sour cream.

Variations: other fruits such as mandarin sections, chopped walnuts, sliced green olives and 1 tablespoon cottage cheese may be included. This salad is a traditional favorite with potlucks and church suppers.

Chickpea (garbanzo) Salad

1 can chickpeas

½ carrot, cut up

1 scallion, sliced

⅛ cup red onion, sliced

Red bell pepper, 6-8 slices

1 roma tomato, sliced

1 teaspoon cumin seeds, toasted

Parsley, dill, chives to taste

Salt and pepper to taste

Dressing: olive oil and sherry, red wine or balsamic vinegar 2:1.

This hearty salad can be a main dish paired with a good bread with cheese. Or feta cheese may be sprinkled on the salad.

Edamame Salad

¼ cup edamame, cooked and cooled

1 green onion

4 slices avocado

¼ cup cooked brown rice

¼ teaspoon ginger root, chopped or grated

Dressing:

1 teaspoon soy sauce

½ teaspoon sesame oil

1 teaspoon rice vinegar

1 teaspoon mirin

Basil leaves or shiso leaf

This is an excellent and not so common salad.

Asparagus with Sesame Tahini

5-6 spears asparagus

Cut off tough ends, steam or boil but do not overcook. Cool.

Dressing:

1 tablespoon sesame tahini

¼ teaspoon soy sauce

¼ teaspoon rice vinegar

Scant teaspoon sugar

Combine dressing ingredients and serve as a dip with asparagus spears.

If this recipe is expanded for guests it is always a hit, especially as it is not so common. This dip can also be used for other raw vegetables such as carrots, celery, or snow peas. Sesame tahini is often used in Japanese cuisine.

Wild Rice Salad

1 cup cooked wild rice or a combination of wild and brown rice

4 walnuts, chopped

2 tablespoons dried cranberries

2 tablespoons yellow bell pepper, chopped

1 green onion, chopped

Mix all ingredients and dress.

Dressing: Use rice vinegar, sherry vinegar or red wine vinegar. Oil is not necessary for this salad.

When I cook rice I prepare more than one serving. Other varieties of rice, for example, red or pink, or other grains may also be used in salads.

Avocado and Grapefruit Salad

1 grapefruit, sectioned

1 avocado, peeled and sliced

Arrange grapefruit slices alternating with avocado slices on arugula or endive leaves on an attractive plate.

Dress with raspberry vinaigrette, which can be made by adding a bit of raspberry jelly or jam to your vinaigrette. This is another of my favorites and is refreshing and popular with guests. Europeans, unlike Americans, serve salad after the main course so that one's enzymes are not depleted before the entree.

Artichoke Heart and Cauliflower Salad

1 can marinated artichoke hearts

Cauliflower sections, cut up

2-3 mushrooms, sliced

Romaine lettuce

Feta or blue cheese, scattered over ingredients

Several black olives, sliced or whole

2 teaspoons balsamic or white wine vinegar

Dressing: Use oil from artichoke hearts with vinegar and add herbs, such as dill, basil and/or thyme.

Tuna Salad

⅓ can Albacore tuna

½ celery stalk, chopped

1 green onion, sliced

1 small roma tomato, sliced

Dressing: combine all ingredients with home-made mayonnaise to which a bit of chopped garlic may be added. This old standby is often used as a sandwich filling. Parsley and thyme are a good addition to this salad.

Salmon Salad

1 small can Alaskan salmon

1 scallion or 2 green onions, chopped

½ celery stalk, sliced

1 tablespoon yellow bell pepper, chopped

Parsley and pepper to taste

Dressing: your own mayonnaise, which includes lemon juice.

Variation: pineapple, sliced or crushed may be used instead of yellow bell pepper. If you use pineapple be sure not to use fresh fruit as it will dissolve the fish. Fresh cooked salmon may be used instead of canned fish, but canned salmon works better in a salad.

Salmon Mousse (for two)

½ small can of salmon

1 tablespoon gelatin

1 cup hot water

1 teaspoon sugar

2 teaspoons lemon juice

½ stalk celery, chopped

1 green onion or scallion, chopped

Dissolve gelatin in 2 tablespoons cold water, then add hot water, sugar and lemon juice. Cool, then add other ingredients and pour into mold. Chill. Dress with mayonnaise, mixed with a bit of dill.

Malaysian Salad

Cucumber, 5 slices

Jicama, 5 slices

⅓ cup fresh bean sprouts

5 pineapple cubes

Combine ingredients and dress.

Dressing:

1 teaspoon soy sauce

½ teaspoon sesame oil

1 teaspoon rice vinegar

½ teaspoon sugar

Combine all dressing ingredients and dress salad.

Tofu Edamame Salad

6 cubes tofu

8 cooked edamame

1 roma tomato, sliced

½ teaspoon ginger root, grated

Dressing:

1 teaspoon soy sauce

½ teaspoon rice vinegar

1 teaspoon mirin (or sugar)

Combine dressing ingredients with ginger root and dress salad.

Mushroom and Pea Salad

¼ cup sliced white mushrooms

¼ cup sliced shiitake mushrooms, sliced

1 tablespoon butter

1 green onion

¼ cup frozen peas

Sauté mushrooms in butter until tender. In a separate pan steam or boil peas briefly and combine with mushrooms and green onion.

Dressing:

1 teaspoons soy sauce

Pepper to taste

1 teaspoon mirin be added for a sweeter salad.

½ teaspoon oil

Green Papaya Salad

1 green papaya

½ semi-green mango, sliced

Peel, seed and slice papaya very thin. Sprinkle with salt and let stand till soft. Add cold water and squeeze out liquid. Mango should be added before salting.

Dressing: vinegar and sugar only.

Variation: add fresh hot chili pepper to taste if desired. This salad is popular in Hawai'i and parts of Southeast Asia.

Wakame Snow Pea Salad

A few shreds of wakame

6 snow peas

2 tablespoons slivered carrot

Lightly steam snow peas for 1 minute. Dissolve wakame shreds in boiling water but do not boil. Drain and cool wakame. Combine with peas and carrot slivers.

Dressing:

1 teaspoon sesame oil

1 teaspoon soy sauce

½ teaspoon rice vinegar

½ teaspoon mirin

This unusual salad may be a hit with guests who are not too staid in their tastes. Try this same recipe with potato instead of snow peas. It makes an unusual potato salad.

Fennel Salad

½ a fennel bulb, cored, stalks removed

1 chamomile tea bag

1 ½ tablespoon white wine vinegar

½ teaspoon chopped fresh rosemary

3 tablespoons olive oil

¼ teaspoon salt

¼ teaspoon freshly ground pepper

Thinly slice fennel diagonally and place in a bowl. In a small bowl steep chamomile tea bag in vinegar 15 minutes. Squeeze out tea bag into bowl, discard bag. Add rosemary to vinegar/tea mixture and whisk with olive oil, salt and pepper. Drizzle dressing over fennel and refrigerate until read to serve. Multiply by four for four servings. This licorice flavored salad is always a favorite. Some chopped celery may also be added.

[III]

SAUCES, DIPS AND DRESSINGS

Dressings, sauces and dips can be created in endless variety, depending only on the imagination of the chef. A dressing can make a salad unique, just as a sauce can make a piece of fish or a quinoa dish distinctive. Some ingredients I regard as essential in my larder for these enhancements.

For oils I keep extra virgin olive oil and toasted sesame oil always on hand. For certain dressings I sometimes also keep peanut oil or macadamia nut oil available.

For vinegar I use five basic varieties: red wine, white wine, balsamic, sherry and rice wine vinegars and always have them in my larder. Occasionally I also use pear or raspberry vinegar, which can be a refreshing alternative to the above, especially in a fruit salad. Many chefs like cider vinegar or champagne vinegar, so the goal is not to limit possibilities. Other ingredients to keep handy in dips and sauces are miso and tahini, both of which I use often. I also use ginger root, garlic, mirin (sweet sake), and shoyu liberally in my cuisine, and often these are essential in dips and sauces. I'm fond of olives, both black and green varieties, and often these feature in my dips or sauces, as well as in soups and fish dishes.

In addition to the above ingredients, vegetables are often components of dips or sauces, either in pureed form or in pieces, as in a spinach dip, paired with yogurt, sour cream, mayonnaise. or a combination of the three. Of course herbs and spices always enhance flavors.

The recipes included here are suggestions for a cook, whether experienced or aspiring and are by no means exhaustive of the possibilities. As with other sections of this book, my approach has been influenced by having lived in India, Japan and Southeast Asia for extended periods of time. For example, in my larder I keep the basic ingredients of a good curry: cumin, coriander, cardamom, turmeric, fenugreek, asafetida, red chilies, and coconut milk. Let's begin by considering the creation of dressings.

Basic Mayonnaise

1 teaspoon lemon juice

1 teaspoon salt

1 teaspoon mustard

1 egg, beaten

1 cup canola oil

Place the first four ingredients in a small blender and blend while gradually adding the canola oil. This is one instance where olive oil does not work as well as canola oil. Place in a jar with a lid and refrigerate. This is easy to make and will last quite well in the refrigerator.

Variation: For a basic aioli use 1 tablespoon of this mayonnaise mixed with half a teaspoon or more of chopped garlic. This makes an excellent dip for chilled asparagus, artichokes, or green beans. It is best after being refrigerated overnight.

Basic Vinaigrette

¼ cup olive oil

¼ cup vinegar

½ teaspoon salt

Pepper to taste

Not all cooks agree on the proportion of oil to vinegar. Some use a ratio of 2 to 1, 3 or even 4 to 1, but I like a nippy dressing, so I use a larger proportion of vinegar. This is just the basic recipe and can be varied in infinite variety. Try using different vinegars or fruit juices for this dressing.

Variations: From there, you can add mustard, honey, dill, cilantro, basil, raspberry juice, or whatever strikes your fancy. Honey and mustard make the vinaigrette an especially good pairing with a green salad. The point is that this dressing is so easy to make and store that I seldom resort to buying ready-made dressing. For an Oriental salad I generally prefer toasted sesame oil and rice vinegar, but there is no hard and fast rule.

Miso Tahini Dressing

2 tablespoons white miso

1 tablespoon tahini

2 tablespoons fresh lemon juice

3 tablespoons water

½ tablespoon honey

1 teaspoon fresh chopped dill

¼ teaspoon turmeric

Stir miso and tahini together in a bowl. Add lemon juice and water and mix well. Add all other ingredients. This is a thick, creamy, tangy dressing that goes well on greens wilted in sesame oil, shoyu, and water with a bit of chopped red bell pepper. You might like to try it with avocado added to the greens. You could also use it as a dip, with a bit less water.

Orange Sesame Dressing

2 tablespoons orange juice

½ teaspoon rice vinegar

2 tablespoons sesame oil

½ teaspoon shoyu

¼ teaspoon roasted sesame seeds

½ teaspoon grated ginger root

½ teaspoon chopped garlic

Combine all in a covered jar and shake well.

Variations: Add ¼ teaspoon Dijon mustard. Try cranberry juice or pomegranate juice in place or orange juice in this dressing, though these additions make it lose some of its Oriental flavor.

Poppy Seed Dressing

    2 tablespoons olive oil

    2 teaspoons lemon juice

    1 teaspoon honey

    ½ teaspoon poppy seeds

Mix together, place in a covered jar and shake until thoroughly mixed. This dressing is especially suited to a fruit salad, for example, avocado-grapefruit, arranged alternately on a plate with the dressing drizzled over it.

Variation: For 2 teaspoons lemon juice, try 1 teaspoon lemon juice and 1 teaspoon pear vinegar.

Sesame-Tahini Dip

1 tablespoon sesame tahini

½ teaspoon shoyu

½ teaspoon rice vinegar

1 teaspoon sugar

Mix all together. This is an excellent dip for chilled asparagus, artichoke, or green beans, and is always a hit. If you serve it to guests, they will almost always ask for the recipe. This is enough for one serving, so for guests simply multiply. This dip should be quite firm, not mushy. The vegetables should also be firm enough that they don't collapse when dipped.

Hummus

1 can garbanzos (chick peas), drained

1-2 cloves garlic, chopped

5 tablespoons sesame tahini   4 tablespoons chopped parsley

¼ cup olive oil   Salt, pepper, cayenne, and

3-4 tablespoons lemon juice   cumin to taste

Place all ingredients in a blender and blend to a thick paste. For a coarser texture, the garbanzos can be mashed by hand with the other ingredients. Keep in a lidded jar in the refrigerator. Hummus can be served on toast, crackers, or as a dip with raw vegetables.

You might even try some over rice or noodles.

Sweet Red Pepper Sauce

1 red bell pepper	Salt and pepper to taste
2 cloves garlic	2 tablespoons chopped parsley
2 tablespoons olive oil	1 tablespoon fresh dill weed
⅓ cup vegetable stock	

Roast garlic wrapped in foil 25 minutes in 350 degree oven. Roast red pepper then peel and seed when cooled. Chop pepper and add with other ingredients to a blender. Puree. Add a pinch of cayenne if desired. This sauce is excellent over toast, polenta, or some white fish. Over polenta add sautéed portabella mushrooms. The sauce is also tasty over Quorn, the commercially available chicken substitute.

A similar sauce can be made with other vegetables, for example, cooked carrots with an addition of orange zest and cumin.

Sake-shoyu Marinade

¼ cup sake

2 teaspoons shoyu

2 teaspoons mirin

Place in a heavy frying pan and use for marinating and poaching fish. I nearly always cook salmon this way. This recipe is for one salmon cutlet. Other cooks prefer to serve salmon with a mayonnaise-dill dressing with lemon juice, but this recipe is my personal favorite and it gives the fish an Oriental touch. Some recipes also call for serving salmon with various salsas.

Cilantro-Capers Marinade

½ cup chopped fresh cilantro

1 tablespoon capers

2 tablespoons fresh lime juice

This marinade is also excellent for a mild white fish such as tilapia or sole. Combine the marinade with the fish in foil, and bake in a 350 degree oven until the fish is cooked through, about 15 minutes. Fish can also be cooked in a heavy frying pan with this marinade. Chopped olives are an excellent addition to this marinade.

Japanese Marinade for Vegetables

1 cup liquid, stock made with dashi and kombu

(see recipe for miso in the Soup chapter)

2 tablespoons shoyu

1 tablespoon mirin

Boil vegetables, including carrots, green beans, daikon, bamboo shoots, snow peas and shiitake mushrooms in this marinade. Vegetables prepared this way are served cold, Japanese style, called *nishime.* Japanese cooks add some kinds of mountain potatoes and taro. Sweet potatoes are also suitable for this preparation.

Sauce Verde

⅓ cup packed basil leaves

1 tablespoon fresh lemon juice

1 green onion, chopped

2 teaspoons Dijon mustard

2 tablespoons packed parsley

1 garlic clove, chopped

1 tablespoon drained capers

2 tablespoons olive oil

Blend all chopped vegetables with lemon juice and gradually add the olive oil.

This sauce is excellent over green beans, zucchini, or even carrots.

Variation: Try cilantro, about 2 tablespoons, instead of basil.

Pesto

1 cup packed basil leaves

1 clove garlic, chopped

1 tablespoon olive oil

2 tablespoons parmesan or mozzarella cheese, crumbled

1-2 tablespoons pine nuts or walnuts

Sauté nuts and garlic briefly. Mix all ingredients either by hand or in a blender. Serve over noodles or spaghetti.

Variations: I like to add a bit of butter to the pesto. Or you can use the olive oil-butter combination commercially available. You can also try cilantro instead of basil and raw almonds instead of pine nuts, with a teaspoon of lemon juice.

Curry Dip

1 teaspoon curry powder

1 tablespoon sour cream

1 tablespoon mayonnaise

1 teaspoon toasted cumin seeds

Mix all ingredients together and serve as a dip with raw vegetables. This recipe is adequate for one or possibly two servings.

Variation: Of course you can make the curry powder from scratch, using cumin, coriander, cardamom, turmeric, and cayenne or red pepper flakes.

Eggplant Dip

1 eggplant, skin pierced

½ medium onion, chopped

1 tablespoon capers

2 tablespoons fresh lemon juice

½ teaspoon dried oregano

Salt, freshly ground black pepper

1 teaspoon red wine vinegar

1 tomato, peeled, seeded, diced

1 tablespoon fresh chopped parsley

Pierce and bake eggplant 30 minutes. Peel and blend, adding onions, capers and lemon juice. Gradually add olive oil while blending. Stir in vinegar, salt, pepper and oregano. Add parsley before serving in warm pitas, cut into wedges. This dip is also called Baba Ganouch and can be used with chips.

Spinach Dip

1 small shallot, peeled, chopped	Salt and pepper to taste
½ cup cream cheese	6 ounces baby spinach
¼ cup yogurt	2 tablespoons chopped chives
2 teaspoons lemon juice	

Place all in a blender and blend together. This dip is used for chips or crackers, or sometimes for raw vegetables.

Variation: Add ¼ cup chopped ripe olives and ¼ cup salsa. Cream cheese and chopped black olives alone make a tasty spread for toast or sandwiches.

White Bean Dip

1 15 ounce can cannellini beans

2 tablespoons olive oil

3 garlic cloves, sliced

1 bay leaf

2 teaspoons thyme leaves

Warm olive oil and add garlic, bay leaf and thyme. Stir for 3 or 4 minutes until garlic browns. Pour hot oil over beans and stir. Garnish with another teaspoon of olive oil, salt and pepper to taste. Store in refrigerator in a covered jar. Serve with crackers or flat bread.

Variations: Sage or rosemary may be substituted for bay leaf and thyme.

Lentil Walnut Paté

2 teaspoons olive oil

2 tablespoons minced onion

½ cup cooked lentils, water removed

2 tablespoons chopped walnuts

½ teaspoon lemon juice

1 tablespoon mayonnaise

1 tablespoon chopped parsley

Salt and pepper to taste

Dash of cayenne

Sauté onion in olive oil in a skillet over medium heat until slightly brown. Mash and add lentils, then walnuts, mayonnaise, lemon juice and seasonings and blend. Serve with crackers or chips.

Variation: white wine may be used instead of lemon juice.

Mushroom Almond Paté

2 tablespoons chopped onion	3 tablespoons almonds, ground
2 teaspoons chopped garlic	1 teaspoon thyme
1 tablespoon butter	Salt and pepper to taste
4 mushrooms, chopped	1 ½ tablespoons sherry

Sauté onions and garlic in butter until translucent. Add chopped mushrooms and cook until soft. Add sherry then reduce the liquid. Add salt, pepper and thyme to taste, them almond meal. Mix and serve either warm or cold with crackers and/or chips. This is excellent with a sip of sherry.

Variation: Marsala may be substituted for sherry.

Tofu Dip

5 ounces silken or soft tofu

1 tablespoon oil

1 tablespoon lemon juice

2 teaspoons parsley flakes

1 tablespoon minced dill pickles

2 teaspoons minced onion

¼ teaspoon mustard

Combine all in a food processor and blend until smooth. This dip can also be used as a tangy mayonnaise, for example in potato salad.

Walnut Sauce

2-3 tablespoons chopped walnuts

2 teaspoons butter

½ teaspoon garlic, chopped

1 teaspoon rosemary

1 teaspoon parsley

1 teaspoon white wine

Sauté walnuts in butter until crisp and add garlic, rosemary and parsley and cook another minute. Finish sauce with white wine. Serve over pasta or stuffed ravioli.

Variation: Other walnut recipes call for a creamy sauce over pastas. This recipe includes milk, olive oil, and ricotta cheese but no wine. Sometimes butter is used rather than olive oil.

Béchamel Sauce

2 tablespoons butter

2 tablespoons flour

2 cups milk

1 teaspoon salt

¼ teaspoon grated nutmeg

Melt the butter in a heavy pan, then whisk in the flour gradually, cooking for about 6 minutes. The gradually add the milk, whisking with each addition. Add the salt and nutmeg when the mixture thickens. This sauce can be used for lasagna and other cheese, pasta, and polenta preparations. With the addition of an egg and a fourth of a cup of mozzarella or Parmesan it becomes Alfredo sauce.

[IV]

LEGUMES

Legumes are a staple of a vegetarian and also a Mediterranean and an Indian diet, and they come in infinite variety. There are kidney beans, black beans, green beans, navy beans, cannellini beans, garbanzo beans, fava beans, lima beans, mung beans, adzuki beans, anasazi beans, edamame, and this doesn't even exhaust the possibilities. Then there are lentils—yellow, red, green, and brown,

Peas are also legumes—snow peas, snap peas, black eyed peas, and no doubt others. When combined with rice, as in Mexican cuisine, beans constitute a perfect protein, and even without rice they are rich in protein. The only caveat is that I discovered that some people are unable to eat fava beans, myself among them.

Legumes contain less fat and cholesterol than meat and lend themselves to combination with other vegetables and with a variety of sauces as well as with grains. Legumes are therefore a healthful way to include protein in the diet.

To avoid the unpleasant after-effects of eating beans affecting many people, carefully wash the beans and soak them in cold water at least four hours. The longer they are soaked the more easily digested they will be. If you change the water several times during soaking, the after-effects will be further diminished. Let's explore a few recipes using legumes. Since many of these recipes involve a can of beans or soaking beans before cooking, these recipes typically serve more than one.

Walnut Lentil Burgers

½ cup cooked, drained lentils

3 tablespoons chopped walnuts

1 teaspoon vinegar

1 teaspoon olive oil

2 tablespoons chopped onion

1 clove chopped garlic

1-2 chopped mushrooms

Salt and pepper to taste

1 tablespoon bread crumbs

½ teaspoon mustard

Sauté onion in a skillet until translucent. Add all remaining ingredients except bread crumbs and sauté about 8 minutes, or until tender. Add bread crumbs and mix well.

Chill before forming the burger. Fry on both sides in a bit of oil. Serve with slices of ripe tomatoes, salsa, or tofu dip with mustard. This makes a single serving.

Dhal

½ cup yellow or red lentils	¼ teaspoon cumin
2 cups water	1 tablespoon oil
1 tablespoon onion, chopped	⅛ teaspoon red pepper
Dash of turmeric	½ teaspoon salt
1 teaspoon lemon juice	

Soak lentils in water overnight or at least four hours. Then bring to a boil, lower heat and simmer covered about half an hour or until soft.

Sauté onions in oil in a skillet until they begin to brown, then add cumin, red pepper, and turmeric. Fry about one minute, then add the mixture to lentils and continue simmering about 20 minutes, adding lemon and salt.

Some cooks like a more liquid dhal, almost a soup, others like a firmer mix. Thickness can of course be adjusted by the amount of water used. This is a staple in Indian cuisine and is often mixed with basmati rice. This recipe serves one or two people.

Variation: spinach, a tomato, or acorn squash cubes may be added. Dhal can also be made with garbanzos rather than lentils.

Garbanzo Curry

1 can garbanzos	2 tablespoons chopped onion
1 tablespoon oil	1 small clove garlic, chopped
1 small tomato	Dash of chopped green chili
½ teaspoon cumin	¼ teaspoon coriander
Dash of turmeric	Dash of red pepper
Dash of cinnamon	Dash of cloves
Dash of pepper	½ teaspoon. salt
2 tablespoons water	½ teaspoon lemon juice

Sauté onion and garlic in oil. When onions begin to brown add tomato, green chili, and spices, mixed together. Fry 2-5 minutes. Add garbanzos, salt, and water and stir. Remove from heat and add lemon juice. This is another staple of the Indian diet.

Variation: 1 cup of chopped mushrooms may be added with garbanzos. This is called channa curry. Tomatoes and red or yellow bell peppers are another possible addition

Garbanzo Burgers

½ can garbanzos	1 teaspoon chopped garlic
½ teaspoon cumin	Fresh parsley leaves
Dash red pepper flakes	¼ teaspoon lemon juice
2 teaspoons flour	Arugula leaves, stems removed
Salt and pepper to taste	2 teaspoons oil

Place all except flour in processor and blend. Stir in flour and salt and shape into burgers. Fry on both sides in oil 3 minutes.

Garnish with red pepper sauce or salsa.

Boston Baked Beans

1 cup canned Great Northern beans	¼ teaspoon dry mustard
Large onion slice stuck with 2 cloves	¼ teaspoon ground ginger
¼ cup molasses	¼ teaspoon salt
⅓ cup dark brown sugar	Pepper to taste
1 cup water	

Combine all except beans, whisk, and pour over beans. Bake in a Dutch oven 250 Degrees for 1 hour. Since this is a Fourth of July or pot luck favorite, the recipe can be multiplied 2 or more times.

Vegetarian Chili

1 can kidney beans

1 onion, chopped

1 tomato, chopped

1 garlic clove, chopped

2 tablespoons yellow bell pepper, chopped

2 mushrooms, chopped

2 tablespoons. oil

1 teaspoon paprika

Dash of salt and pepper

2 teaspoons chili powder

Sugar to taste

Sauté onion and bell pepper in oil, then add garlic, followed by tomato.

Add beans, paprika, and chili powder. Simmer 15 minutes, adding water if necessary. Add salt and sugar to taste. Garnish with cilantro and, if desired, sour cream.

Tomatoes may also be added.

Lentil and Vegetable Casserole

½ cup red lentils

¼ cup onion, chopped

1 tablespoon oil

2 teaspoons chopped garlic

1 celery stalk, sliced

1 large carrot, sliced

1 small leek, sliced

2 cups stock or water

1/teaspoon lemon juice

Salt and pepper to taste

Soak lentils 4 hours, then simmer 30 minutes or till soft. Sauté onion, celery, then garlic in oil. Add carrot, leek, and stock and simmer Stir in cooked lentils. Season with lemon juice, salt and pepper.

Variation: green beans and peas may be added. To make a spicier dish, add cayenne, cumin, coriander and turmeric. Garnish with parsley or cilantro.

Lima Bean Casserole

1 cup cooked baby lima beans	1 stalk celery, sliced
½ cup corn kernels	1 tomato, diced
1 tablespoon onion, chopped	1 clove garlic, minced
½ teaspoon thyme	½ teaspoon basil
1 tablespoon chopped leek	1 small bay leaf
or green onion	1 tablespoon oil
Salt and pepper to taste	

Sauté onion, leek, then garlic in oil. When onion begins to brown, add celery, and cook 3 minutes more. Then add tomato, bay leaf, corn kernels and cooked limas. Add a bit of water only if necessary. Add thyme, basil, and salt and pepper to taste. Remove the bay leaf before serving with parsley or cilantro garnish.

Variation: black-eyed peas can be used for this recipe in place of lima beans. Black-eyed peas need to be soaked in water and cooked until tender.

Adzuki Beans and Sweet Potatoes

⅓ cup dry adzuki beans

1 sweet potato, peeled and cubed

3 cups water

1 small onion, chopped

1 garlic clove, minced

1 carrot, peeled and sliced

1 teaspoon ginger, peeled & grated

1 teaspoon tamari

Cayenne and salt to taste

Rinse beans and place in a pot with water. Simmer partially covered.

Sauté onion and garlic in oil. Then add sweet potato and carrots. Cook over high heat and when nearly done add cooked beans and ginger. Continue to cook until vegetables are soft. Season with cayenne and tamari.

Peas with Mint

1 cup peas in the pod, shelled

2 teaspoons butter

Bit of orange zest

2 tablespoons fresh mint leaves, chopped

2 teaspoons scallions, chopped

Boil peas in slightly salted water until bright green and tender, 2 minutes.

Drain. Toss with butter and orange zest, mint and scallions. Salt to taste. Mint is a tasty accompaniment to peas, either in this form or in soups.

[V]

OTHER VEGETABLES

Recipes in this chapter are intended to include vegetables other than legumes, though some recipes may also include a type of bean. Greens, root vegetables, and any others will be featured here. Since this book's approach is basically pescetarian or Mediterranean, it is important to consider the protein content of vegetables other than legumes. A later chapter will feature eggs, cheese, and tofu recipes in order to ensure an adequate protein component in one's diet. My recipes are often influenced by Indian or Japanese seasonings. Local seasonal availability influences our choice of what to cook, with root vegetables prominent in fall and winter and greens available in spring and summer. If you are fortunate enough to have space to grow your own vegetables, then you can ensure that you are not eating compromised food. Organic selections are often a good alternative, although even they are not always necessarily additive-free.

Some of these recipes will be enough to serve two or maybe three, depending on your appetite. As in other chapters, when oil is an ingredient, I prefer extra virgin olive oil, unless otherwise specified. Grapeseed oil is another good choice.

Indian Mixed Vegetables (Navratan Curry)

1 small carrot	1 small potato
2 tablespoons green beans	2 tablespoons peas
1 small onion	1 scallion
1 tablespoon oil	½ teaspoon cumin
¼ teaspoon coriander	Dash of turmeric
1 cherry tomato	1 mushroom
2 tablespoons yogurt	Dash of cayenne
Salt and pepper	

Sauté onion and scallion in oil until they begin to brown. Add cumin, coriander, cayenne and turmeric and cook 1 minute. Peel and boil potato and carrot and add with beans and peas to mixture. Continue to cook until vegetables are cooked firm. Add yogurt and salt and pepper to taste. This recipe serves two.

Variation: cauliflower is often included in this Narrating curry, but I generally avoid including strong vegetables such as turnips or parsnips in this preparation.

Vegetarian Chili

1 cup cooked kidney beans	1 stalk celery
⅓ cup corn kernels	½ cup chopped yellow bell pepper
3 cherry tomatoes	1 tablespoon oil
¼ cup sliced carrot	1 teaspoon cumin
¼ seeded, chopped jalapeno pepper	Dash of cayenne
2 teaspoons raw sugar	1 teaspoon salt
2 tablespoons chopped onion	

Sauté onion, celery and bell pepper in oil. Add cumin, chopped jalapeno, and cayenne and sauté 1 more minute. Add tomatoes, cut in half, partially cooked carrot slices, corn, and kidney beans and cook covered on low heat for 30 minutes. Salt to taste and add sugar. Sugar gives this chili its distinctively sweet flavor, not always associated with chili.

Potato Cauliflower Curry

1 medium potato, cubed	6-7 cauliflower flowerets
2 tablespoons chopped onion	1 scallion
1 medium tomato, blanched	1 teaspoon cumin seeds
peeled and diced	1 teaspoon coriander
¼ teaspoon turmeric	1 tablespoon oil
1/teaspoon lemon juice	1 teaspoon mustard seeds

Sauté mustard seeds in oil in a skillet until they pop. Add cumin seeds and sauté 1 or 2 minutes. Add onion, scallion, coriander, turmeric and tomato and cook 2 minutes. Then add potato and cauliflower pieces and cook covered on low heat for 10 to 15 minutes. Add a bit of water if necessary. Garnish with parsley or coriander and add lemon juice.

Variation: For a hotter curry, add 1 teaspoon green chilies, seeded and chopped and 1 teaspoon chopped ginger root with the spices during cooking. Yogurt is also optional.

Stuffed Green Peppers

1 large green pepper	⅓ cup cooked rice
2 teaspoons onion, chopped	1 mushroom, sliced
6 edamame	2 teaspoons oil
Salt and pepper to taste	Bits of tomato

Remove the top of the bell pepper and scrape out the insides.

Sauté onion, mushroom, and edamame in oil for 3 minutes. Add the few tomato pieces, cooked rice, salt and pepper to the mixture and stuff the pepper. Place water in the bottom of an 8 x 8 inch pan, put the pepper in the pan and the pan in the oven. Bake 350 degrees for 30 minutes, or alternatively, cook the pepper in the top of a double boiler until tender. If you have a large enough Japanese bamboo steamer this is also a good way to cook this pepper or in fact any other vegetable not being fried.

Variation: To add spice, shake a few pepper flakes into the rice mixture.

Sweet Potatoes and Parsnips

1 medium sweet potato	1 large parsnip
1-2 tablespoons butter	Salt and pepper to tastes
2 cups water	

Peel and slice potato and parsnip and cook in simmering water until tender.

Mash together and add butter, salt and pepper to taste.

If you like parsnips, this simple recipe is excellent. I don't even add an herb garnish.

Variation: I sometimes add some carrot to the mixture, which is also delicious. Or you can try adding a tablespoon of orange juice and parsley garnish before serving.

Cilantro is an acceptable garnish for most vegetable dishes.

Asparagus and Artichokes

See chapter three for the sesame tahini dip for chilled asparagus and also chapter three for the aioli dip for chilled artichokes. These are my favorite ways to enjoy these two spring vegetables. Their flavors are so distinctive that I don't mix them with other vegetables. Some prefer artichoke served hot, in which case you may prefer to dip it in butter.

Zucchini with Bell Pepper

1 medium zucchini, sliced	½ green or red bell pepper
2 teaspoons onion, chopped	1 teaspoon garlic, chopped
1 tablespoon oil	1 green onion or chives
1 teaspoon marjoram leaves	Salt and pepper to taste
1 teaspoon basil leaves	

Sauté onion, chives and garlic in oil. Add chopped zucchini, bell pepper, basil and marjoram and continue cooking until tender. Add salt and pepper to taste.

Variation: Tarragon is sometimes used with zucchini but it is difficult to combine with other herbs as it overpowers them. Parsley can be used to garnish and grated parmesan is also a good garnish. I enjoy a cilantro garnish for most vegetable.

Harvard Beets

1 or 2 beets	1 teaspoon dill
4 cup water	1 teaspoon lemon thyme
1 teaspoon red wine vinegar	1 teaspoon cornstarch
Dash of mustard	½ teaspoon sugar

Boil unpeeled beets in water until tender. Do not discard the water. Then peel and slice the beets. In a skillet place ½ cup of the water and add cornstarch and cook until thickened. Add the beets, dill, lemon thyme, and vinegar and mix to coat the beets.

Add the sugar and a dash of mustard.

Variation: You may also add a bit of butter to the mixture. Serving these beets with greens is both colorful and flavorful. When in a hurry it is always possible to use canned beets, my personal favorite among canned vegetables.

Spinach, Kale, and Chard

1-2 cups packed greens

1 cup water

1 teaspoon white wine vinegar

Any of these greens, which I don't necessarily cook together, need only be wilted in boiling water or alternatively, in oil in a skillet. Add the vinegar before serving. The vinegar can be infused with hot peppers if desired. I keep a small bottle of chili-infused vinegar in my refrigerator.

Variation: My favorite way of cooking greens is to wilt them with a bit of butter in a skillet, add a sliced mushroom, then finish with a generous teaspoon of sake, cooking for another minute. These leafy vegetables are especially packed with nutrition and should be included in one's diet whenever possible.

Broccoli with Cheese

6-7 broccoli flowerets

1 tablespoon chopped onion

1 cup water

2 teaspoons oil

Salt and pepper to taste

1 teaspoon chopped garlic

2 tablespoons cream

2 tablespoons grated Parmesan,

cheddar or mozzarella cheese

Boil broccoli in water until tender. Sauté onion in oil until it begins to brown, then add garlic and cook another 1-2 minutes. Turn heat low, add cream and cheese to melt but not boil. For more sauce, add a bit of water and cornstarch, with more cheese. Add broccoli to mixture, season, and serve over rice. Garnish with cilantro or parsley.

Saag (Spinach- Indian)

1 package frozen spinach

½ teaspoon grated ginger

1 small garlic clove, chopped

¼ teaspoon green chili, seeded & chopped

¼ teaspoon garam masala

Pinch of fenugreek leaves, crumbled

2-3 tablespoons heavy cream

Salt to taste

1 tablespoon oil or ghee

Thaw the spinach. In a skillet, sauté ginger, garlic, green chili and fenugreek leaves in oil or ghee (clarified butter) with garam masala. Do not cook for over a minute, while stirring constantly. Add the spinach and salt, cover the pan, and cook over low heat for 10-12 minutes with a bit of water. When the spinach is cooked, add cream.

Saag is served in Indian cuisine with paneer, cheese made with milk, but since most Western cooks are not familiar with making paneer, firm tofu cubes are a good substitute.

Variation: Garbanzos can be added to the spinach instead of tofu. This is often also done in Indian restaurants, so it is not just a Western substitution.

Cabbage, Indian Style

1-2 cups shredded cabbage	1 tablespoon chopped onion
¼ teaspoon grated ginger	2 teaspoons chopped garlic
1 tablespoon chopped onion	3 tablespoons thin carrot spears
½ teaspoon cumin seeds	½ teaspoon coriander seeds
½ teaspoon turmeric	Salt and pepper to taste
¼ teaspoon hot green chili	1 tablespoon oil
seeded and chopped	Pinch of asafoetida
¼ teaspoon mustard seeds	

Heat oil in a skillet, add ginger, onion, and garlic and sauté for 1-2 minutes. Then add cumin and coriander seeds, green chili, asafoetida and turmeric and continue cooking for 3 more minutes. Add carrots and shredded cabbage and cook 5 minutes or until vegetables are done. Since cabbage is a strong-flavored vegetable, it goes well with Indian spices.

Vegetable-Nut Korma

2 teaspoons oil	1 tablespoon chopped onion
1 teaspoon chopped garlic	½ teaspoon grated ginger
2 cardamom pods	⅛ teaspoon turmeric
¼ teaspoon cumin	⅛ teaspoon coriander
2 tablespoons coconut cream or milk	⅓ cup water
2 tablespoons ground almonds	1 teaspoon lemon juice
4 cauliflower flowerets	⅓ cup green beans, halved
⅓ cup sliced carrots	1 teaspoon cilantro
Salt and pepper to taste	

Sauté onion in a skillet, followed by garlic, then ginger, crushed cardamom pods, turmeric, cumin, and coriander. Cook 1 minute. Add coconut milk or cream with the water. Stir and add ground almonds and cook 1-2 minutes.

Boil vegetables until tender, discard the water, and add the spice mixture. Reheat and add lemon juice and garnish with cilantro to serve. If you like Indian cuisine you will keep these spices in your larder. Though a bit complex, this recipe is well worth the effort. Serve with basmati rice.

Variation: For a spicier version, add half a teaspoon of chopped, seeded green chilies with the ginger and other spices.

Stuffed Acorn Squash

½ acorn squash, seeded

2 mushrooms, sliced

5-6 edamame

2 teaspoons oil

2 teaspoons chopped chives

1 cherry tomato, quartered

Salt and pepper to taste

¼ teaspoon cumin

Sauté mushrooms and edamame in oil 4-5 minutes. Add cumin, chives and tomato and continue cooking 1-2 minutes. Place ingredients in squash half and bake in 350 degree oven until squash is done. When in a hurry, squash can first be microwaved 3 minutes, cut side down on a pan with a bit of water.

Squash can be stuffed with many different combinations of ingredients. Another version is stuffed with shrimp, a cherry tomato, a 2 Tbsp of coconut milk, and a dash of cayenne and curry powder. Or you can try bell peppers and zucchini with onion and a cherry tomato. Zucchini can also be seeded and stuffed similarly.

[VI]

FISH

This book takes a pescetarian approach to cooking and dining, which means it includes fish recipes and approximates a Mediterranean or traditional Japanese diet. Since the Japanese hold the record for longevity, this is one reason for selecting fish over meat. Moreover, three and a half ounces of fish contains the same amount of protein as three and a half ounces of beef or chicken. Another cogent reason is that meat consumption is not ecologically sustainable; half the agricultural land in the U.S. is devoted to animal feed. Still another issue is that animals are often kept in overcrowded conditions, force fed, and/or they are fed additives harmful to our health. Cattle are fed corn rather than grass, their natural food. If this is not enough to convince readers, American obesity, resulting from eating foods high in cholesterol such as meat and fat, also contributes to the uniquely high incidence of cancer, diabetes, and heart disease in this country.

One caveat is that now our oceans are also polluted, even pre-dating the Gulf oil spill. Also, over-fishing is depleting many traditional fishing grounds. Moreover, fish are not exempt from problems such as mercury and other unhealthy substances. Large fish, for example tuna, have a high mercury content. One solution for uncertainty about whether or not a particular fish is safe to consume is to use a fish guide such as the Monterey Bay fish list, which categorizes fish as Best Choices, Good Alternatives, and

Avoid. There are other lists as well, but the Monterey Bay list is reputable and the one I rely on.

Fish have traditionally been eaten in all parts of the world, particularly countries with coastline access, though other countries have also eaten river fish, and some countries consume fish from both sources. This book includes mostly recipes for ocean fish, and since the approach is close to Mediterranean and traditional Japanese cuisine, some recipes from those countries are included here. As with other food, I have been influenced in my selections by my preference for Japanese and Indian cuisine. In 2008 an article in an issue of *Conde Nast* mentioned that the gourmet capital of the world had shifted from Paris to Tokyo. While many Westerners may think of sushi when they think. of Japan, fish is also cooked in various ways that are equally palatable in Japan. See also the recipes in chapter 1, one of which is for bouillabaisse, which includes several varieties of fish and is a Mediterranean soup. Chapter 2 also includes recipes for fish in salads. I generally prefer lobster, salmon or crab in soup or salad.

Good accompaniments for most fish are grains such as rice and quinoa and colorful vegetables such as beets, greens, green beans, and carrots.

Most fish should be seared initially on high heat so that it doesn't lose all its juices, after which the heat should be turned down while it cooks with seasonings.

I always use extra virgin olive oil when cooking fish as well as most vegetables.

Salmon with Sake

1 salmon steak

3 teaspoons sake

2 teaspoons shoyu

1 teaspoon mirin

Marinate salmon steak in the sake, soy sauce, and mirin for half an hour or more.

Heat a skillet and place the marinade in the skillet, then the salmon in the warmed marinade. Poach gently, turning once, until the fish is done, 15 minutes or more. This simple way of preparing salmon is my favorite, as also mentioned in chapter 3. This is a typical method of cooking salmon in Japan. The fish is basically poached.

There are even simpler ways of cooking salmon, for example, simply frying in butter and serving with sour cream or yogurt and dill, or with lemon juice.

Tilapia with Capers

1 tilapia filet

2-3 tablespoons lime juice

1 tablespoon capers

⅓ cup cilantro

Place all ingredients in a skillet with the seasonings covering the fish. Poach gently until the fish is done. Another method of doing this is to place the fish in foil with the seasonings over it and bake in a 350 degree oven. This is also a simple but delicious recipe for fish, and it may be used for sole or other white fish as well. Delicately flavored fish such as tilapia do well with lime juice and capers but less well with strong herbs such as tarragon and rosemary, which overpower the flavor of the fish.

Variation: Olives may also be added to this preparation.

Scallops

4 or 5 scallops

1 scallion or small onion, chopped

1 small tomato, quartered

3 black olives, halved

½ cup white wine

1 teaspoon rosemary or tarragon leaves

1 tablespoon oil

Sauté the onion in oil till light brown, add scallops to sear on one side so they won't overcook. Then add tomato, and wine to poach the fish. When partially done, add the olives and tarragon or rosemary, although the herbs may be added with the tomato. Be careful not to overcook scallops. Since tarragon flavor can overpower others, some may prefer to use thyme or cilantro. If cooking large scallops, three may be enough.

Serve over cooked polenta, rice, or quinoa.

African Shrimp

4-5 large shrimp	2-3 tablespoons peanut butter
2 teaspoons oil	Pinch of red pepper flakes
2 teaspoons chopped onion	Salt and pepper to taste
1 teaspoon chopped garlic	½ teaspoon lemon juice
Pinch of turmeric	1 tablespoon or more of water

Peel and devein shrimp, boiling water for two minutes first if necessary. Sauté onion, followed 3 minutes later by garlic. Mix turmeric, lemon juice, pepper flakes with peanut butter and 1 tablespoon or more of. water. Add shrimp to the onion and garlic, then the peanut butter-spice mixture and cook until the mixture is done, about 8 minutes. If more spices are desired, add half a teaspoon of green chilies to the onion and garlic. Crunchy peanut butter works best with this recipe Serve over rice.

Shrimp Curry

4-5 large shrimp, peeled & deveined

1 small onion or scallion	2 tablespoons coconut milk
1 teaspoon fresh lemon juice	1 teaspoon chopped garlic
Pinch of red pepper flakes	1 small tomato, quartered
$\frac{1}{8}$ teaspoon cumin	$\frac{1}{2}$ teaspoon sugar
2 tablespoons cilantro leaves	$\frac{1}{8}$ teaspoon coriander

Peel and devein shrimp, using boiling water if necessary. Add coconut milk, lemon juice, sugar, tomato, and pepper flakes to the shrimp, mixing well and allow to marinate. In a skillet sauté onion and garlic. Before garlic begins to brown add cumin and coriander to the onion and garlic. Then add the shrimp and coconut milk mixture to the skillet and cook 6 or 7 minutes until the shrimp are done. Serve over basmati rice. Garnish with lemon wedges and cilantro.

Variation: a tablespoon of chopped red bell pepper may be added to the onion and garlic while sautéing. A curry recipe can be used for chicken or lamb if you consume meat.

Cod with Chanterelles

1 piece of codfish

3 large chanterelles

6-7 edamame

1 shallot, chopped

2 teaspoons oil

1 teaspoon sherry vinegar

Sauté chanterelle mushrooms, shallot, and edamame in oil in a skillet.

After 4-5 minutes, add the cod and continue cooking. When nearly done, add sherry vinegar and cilantro. Serve over risotto. If chanterelles are unavailable, oyster mushrooms may be substituted.

Variation: Cooks can experiment with other herbs such as thyme or rosemary, also white wine vinegar. Capers are another excellent addition to most white fish.

Mushrooms such as shiitake actually have a stronger flavor than chanterelles.

Halibut

1 halibut filet	2 teaspoons oil
2 tablespoons chopped chives	2 teaspoons sherry vinegar
2 tablespoons sliced celery	2 black olives, sliced

Sauté halibut with chives, celery and black olives in oil. Add sherry vinegar and serve with greens and quinoa.

Variation: 1 teaspoon orange zest and 1 teaspoon white wine vinegar is a good alternative to the sherry vinegar. Halibut is a delicately flavored fish and easily be overpowered with capers or herbs such as tarragon. Basil, cilantro, coriander, or dill are good choices if you substitute for olives and if you like to experiment.

Catfish

1 piece of catfish	3 cherry tomatoes, halved
2 teaspoons oil	1 teaspoon garlic, chopped
1 teaspoon capers	Salt and pepper to taste
1 teaspoon white wine	1-2 green olives, sliced

Sauté garlic for 1 minute, then add fish, tomatoes, olives, and capers and cook covered until nearly done, 8 or 9 minutes. Add white wine and continue cooking until the fish is done.

Variation: Basil or tarragon may be added to the seasonings. Tarragon is suited to this recipe, since catfish has a strong flavor.

Tuna with Ginger Sauce

1 tuna steak

1 teaspoon chopped cilantro

2 teaspoons oil

1 teaspoon shoyu

1 teaspoon grated ginger

1 teaspoon mirin

1 tablespoon water

Grill or broil tuna on high heat briefly. Heat a skillet with oil and add ginger. Mix in shoyu, mirin and water and heat 1 minute on high heat. Pour over tuna, and continue cooking until done through. Serve with brown rice. This is Japanese style.

Variation: A distinctive alternative is to serve a tuna steak covered with ¼ cup of Kalamata tapenade with capers and 1 tablespoon of toasted almond slivers.

Home-made Sushi

6-8 slices of sushi salmon or hamachi (yellow tail)

1-2 cups cooked sushi rice

Several strips of nori

Shoyu

Wasabi

Pickled ginger slices

1 teaspoon sugar

½ teaspoon rice vinegar

Cook the rice and set aside. Add vinegar and sugar, mixing and fanning the rice as it cools.

Prepare a very small condiment dish with a dab of wasabi added to soy sauce for dipping the fish. Serve the rice in a single serving bowl. Arrange the sushi on a long plate. Take strips of nori, wrap around a piece of fish dipped in the shoyu, together with a bit of rice, and enjoy the individual wrapped sushi. Serve with miso soup. If sushi appeals to you, this is a simple way to enjoy it at home. You need to keep the ingredients in your larder for Japanese cuisine. It works best with sushi grade salmon. If you have a bamboo rolling mat you can place the nori on it, then add the rice, fish and wasabi and roll the sushi, then cut it, as you see done in restaurants.

Sea Bass with Olives

1 4-5 oz. fish filet

1 ½ tablespoon olive oil

½ teaspoon lemon juice

1 tablespoon chopped celery

2 teaspoons chopped spring onion

½ teaspoon garlic, chopped

2 green olives, sliced

Mix all ingredients in a bowl except fish. Set aside. Place fish skin side down with 2 teaspoons oil in a heated skillet and cook uncovered on high heat for 2-3 minutes. Cover and cook on low heat for another 1-2 minutes, covering with the olive mixture. Sea bass is another fish with a delicate flavor that can be overpowered with tarragon or rosemary.

Scalloped Oyster Casserole

4 ½ cup coarse soda cracker crumbs

4 tablespoons milk

¾ lb. melted butter   ½ teaspoon pepper

1 qt. fresh oysters   ¼ teaspoon nutmeg

1 teaspoon salt   ½ cup oyster liquid

Mix cracker crumbs and butter. Put ⅓ of this mixture in a shallow 9 x 12" casserole. Add ½ the seasonings. Add ½ the oysters, add ⅓ of crumbs and the remaining oysters and seasonings. Add the last ⅓ of crumbs on top. Bake 450 degrees 30 minutes. My mother always served this on Christmas Eve, but I don't know the source of the tradition.

Dover Sole with Mushrooms

1 Dover sole filet

2 teaspoons oil

⅓ cup sliced mushrooms

2 tablespoons sliced onions

2 teaspoons white wine

Sauté onions in oil for 3 minutes, then add mushrooms and fish, cooking for 5 or 6 minutes. Add the white wine last, just before serving. Button, shiitake, oyster, or chanterelle mushrooms may be used. I tend to use mushrooms with most fish, although not always if I include olives.

Maryland Crab Cakes

½ lb. crab meat

⅔ cup cracker or bread crumbs

1 tablespoon chopped green onion

1 tablespoon mayonnaise

½ an egg or substitute

1 tablespoon chopped parsley

1 tablespoon chopped celery

½ teaspoon seafood seasoning

Pepper to taste

1 ½ tablespoon peanut oil

Break apart crab meat, checking for shells. Separately combine crumbs, peppers, onion, parsley, celery, seasoning and pepper. Add to crab, stir in egg, mayonnaise. Taste for adequacy of seasoning. Form patties, flatten, refrigerate covered for 30 minutes. Fry 3 minutes on each side till golden brown. Place on towel lined plate. Serve with lemon and tarter sauce, or cilantro-lime sauce. Makes 4 cakes.

Cilantro-lime sauce: ½ cup each mayo or half mayo and half sour cream or yogurt, 1 teaspoon crushed garlic, 1 teaspoon lime juice, and ½ cup cilantro leaves.

Nut-crusted Tilapia

3-4 ounces tilapia

6 ounces almond crumbs

1 teaspoon shoyu

1 clove garlic

Dash of red pepper

2 teaspoons brown sugar

1 Tablespoon olive oil

Dash of black pepper

Preheat broiler and line cooking sheet with foil. Combine nut crumbs, shoyu, Garlic, sugar, olive oil, and red and black pepper in food processor and blend. Cover fish with a thick coating of the mixture. Place fish on cooking sheet, crust side up. Broil ten minutes of until fish flakes readily.

Variation: Hawaiian Macadamia nuts are delicious in this recipe, though they are more expensive. Other varieties of fish may also be prepared in this way.

[VII]

RICE AND OTHER GRAINS

Rice is the main food, the staff of life, in many parts of the world. The Japanese word for rice is also the word for "meal." Rice exists in amazing variety. The commoner varieties found in most stores include white short and long grain, jasmine, Arborio, sushi, brown, brown and white basmati, red, black, and wild, though wild rice is technically not rice. Apart from these common varieties, there are, for example, twelve varieties of African rice, fourteen varieties of Japanese rice, seventeen varieties of basmati rice, and sixteen varieties of Indian rice, to mention a few. And of course rice can be made into flour for noodles and other Asian foods. Many in developing or Third World countries eat rice and/or noodles more than once daily if they can afford it.

Wheat is obviously also a grain, and wheat is covered in the ingredients in other chapters of this book. Aside from rice and wheat, other grains include spelt, couscous, millet, amaranth, quinoa, bulgur, sorghum, rye, barley, cornmeal, oatmeal, teff, and triticale. For individuals who have Celiac or are otherwise sensitive to wheat, grains such as rice, millet, amaranth, and quinoa are a useful substitute. Any of these grains can be used as cereal, with the addition of fruit, nuts, cream/milk. Rice in nearly any variety, combined with beans of nearly any variety forms a perfect protein. Just add onions, garlic, tomatoes, or any other combination that appeals. In fact, all grains are versatile and may be prepared in a variety of delicious ways. There is no attempt in this chapter to be exhaustive with grain recipes, or with recipes for any other ingredient. Many grains are interchangeable; try substituting a different grain for one in a recipe.

It is not necessary to eat beef in order to have adequate protein in the diet. The dangers of over-consumption of meat have already been mentioned in the introduction. More options for high-protein foods will be explored in the next chapter.

Spanish Rice (Paella)

1 cup basmati rice	1 tomato, peeled & chopped
2 tablespoons olive oil	3 tablespoons cooked green beans
1 cup stock or water	3 tablespoons frozen peas, thawed
4 tablespoons chopped red pepper	2 tablespoons chopped celery
Salt and pepper to taste	Pinch of saffron threads
2 tablespoons slivered almonds	Pinch of asafetida

Heat oil in a pan, add red bell pepper and asafetida, stirring for 1-2 minutes.

Add rice and sauté about 3 minutes. Heat vegetable stock separately, adding the vegetables and seasonings. When stock boils, add rice and simmer covered until tender. Serve in a warmed dish, topped with almonds.

Variation: The *paella* I had in Barcelona contained no peas, beans or celery. It did have tomatoes and a few small shrimp and mussels. Mexican rice is similar, but generally served without seafood.

Italian Risotto

4 cups stock

1 cup arborio rice, rinsed

2 tablespoons olive oil/ butter mixture

½ a chopped onion

1 clove chopped garlic

1 tablespoon Italian flat leaf parsley

2 tablespoons white wine

1 tablespoon lemon juice

Salt and pepper to taste

Heat stock in a medium saucepan over low heat but do not boil.

In a large saucepan heat oil and add onion, garlic, parsley and cook briefly. Add rice, stir and coat with oil, and cook until grains turn pearly white. Then add stock, a bit at a time, stirring continually and cook until rice is tender. If you run out of stock before the rice is completely cooked, add a bit more water and continue simmering. Add wine, lemon juice and seasonings when rice is nearly done.

Variation: This is a simple recipe. I generally add shiitake mushrooms and often edamame and/or white fish or shrimp when rice is nearly cooked. An Italian friend likes to add zucchini and tomatoes.

Biryani (Indian rice with vegetables)

1 cup basmati rice	2 tablespoons oil or butter
1 ⅓ cups water or stock	1 small onion, chopped
½ teaspoon cumin seeds	1 teaspoon coriander
½ cup frozen peas	½ teaspoon minced garlic
½ cup green beans	⅓ cup chopped carrots
¼ teaspoon turmeric	Salt and pepper to taste
¼ teaspoon chopped ginger root	Dash of cayenne pepper

Heat oil over medium heat in a heavy pot. Add cumin seeds and sizzle for 10 seconds. Add carrots, beans, and sauté briefly. Add rinsed rice, turmeric, coriander, ginger and garlic and sauté rice 3 minutes. Add water, bring to a boil, cover, and turn heat low to simmer half an hour or until rice is done.

Variation: A small cubed potato may be added, or the biryani can be made with only peas or beans, or mushrooms in place of the above vegetables. The seasonings are basic to most Indian recipes, often with saffron threads and/or green chilies added.

Basmati-Wild Rice Salad

1 cup cooked rice	2 tablespoons dried cranberries
2 tablespoons chopped green onions	2 tablespoons chopped walnuts
3 tablespoons chopped carrots	3 tablespoons chopped red peppers
1 ⅓ cups water	Rice vinegar to taste

Cook rinsed rice in water, first bringing water to a boil, then adding rice and simmering until done. A rice cooker is a sure-fire way to cook rice. Add all other ingredients, mix, and add vinegar, usually one to two tablespoons.

Variation: Try adding a touch of orange zest or green olives. Yellow peppers may be used instead of red bell peppers. I avoid green peppers in this recipe as the flavor is overpowering. This recipe can of course be doubled for a larger group. As it is, it serves four, or if for yourself, it will keep in the refrigerator for several days. Brown rice may also have used, by itself or in combination with one of the above. This recipe also appears in the chapter on salads, above.

Rice Noodles

1 cup dry rice noodles	4 cups boiling water
½ teaspoon ginger root, chopped	1 garlic clove, chopped
⅓ cup snow peas	⅓ cup coarsely grated carrot
½ teaspoon grated ginger root	½ teaspoon chopped garlic
⅓ cup bean sprouts	2 tablespoons oil
2 tablespoons edamame	1 teaspoon soy sauce
2 teaspoons chopped lemon grass	

Cook noodles in boiling water for about 10 minutes. When done, run cold water over noodles in a colander. In a large heavy pan or wok heat oil, add ginger root and sizzle for 2-3 minutes, then add garlic, carrot, bean sprouts, edamame and peas, and cook until nearly tender. Add soy sauce, mix and add noodles. Stir thoroughly and serve.

Variation: Celery, tofu, and shrimp are also good additions. I like to add a bit of sake or mirin while cooking the vegetables. Try adding peanuts instead of edamame.

Lemon grass with peanuts gives this dish a Southeast Asian touch.

Polenta

1 cup cornmeal

4 cups water

½ teaspoon salt

Bring 3 cups of water to a boil. In another bowl combine cornmeal with the other cup of water and mix until smooth. Add the cornmeal to the boiling water, add salt, and mix until smooth. Then simmer, stirring frequently, until very thick. This basic recipe can be served in a variety of ways, limited only by your imagination.

Variations: When polenta is firm and cooled slightly, cut into serving size pieces and top with your favorite sauce. I like to serve polenta in portabella mushrooms, topped with cheese and olives. Or simply serve topped with grated cheese and sliced tomatoes. Try it with your favorite salsa. You might also try it with pesto or seasoned beans. Of course cornmeal cooked with a higher proportion of water yields cornmeal mush, which is a good breakfast, with fruit and nuts added. Polenta is versatile, although I have never eaten it in a salad.

Couscous with Vegetable Sauce

1 cup couscous	1 ½ cups water
1 tablespoons butter	2 tablespoons chopped onion
1 chopped garlic clove	Salt & pepper to taste

Sauté onion and garlic in oil, add couscous and water and simmer until done.

This dish goes well with a vegetable sauce or salsa

Vegetable Sauce

1 tablespoon butter

1 tomato, 1 small potato cubed

½ cup each edamame, sliced zucchini and green pepper

1 teaspoon each cumin, coriander and turmeric

Salt and pepper to taste

1 cup water

Sauté seasonings briefly in oil, then add vegetables and water and cook until they are tender. Add salt and pepper and serve with a over cooked couscous. Cayenne, lemon grass, and/or hot green chilies may be added to taste.

Couscous Salad

2 cups cooked couscous, as above

1 green onion, sliced

1 cup arugula, cut up

1 tablespoon orange juice

1 tablespoon white wine vinegar

1 teaspoon mustard

2 teaspoons honey

1 tablespoon olive oil

Salt and pepper to taste

2 tablespoons toasted almonds, sliced

Toss cooled couscous with spinach and green onion. In another dish whisk orange juice, vinegar, honey and mustard together. Add olive oil and blend. Pour dressing over couscous salad and top with almonds.

Variation: Try adding half a cup of strawberries or raspberries to the couscous salad before dressing. I tried replacing arugula with spinach and found it delectable.

Quinoa with Mushrooms

½ cup quinoa	1 tablespoon olive oil
4 mushrooms	2 tablespoons cilantro, chopped
⅓ cup garbanzos or edamame	⅓ cup sliced zucchini
Salt and pepper to taste	1 teaspoon chopped garlic
1 teaspoon lemon juice	1 cup water

Cook quinoa in water or stock in a covered pan until done, about 10 minutes. In a separate pan sauté mushrooms and zucchini in oil, adding garlic and beans 3 minutes later. Add the mushroom-zucchini mixture to cooked quinoa. Add lemon juice and fluff the quinoa. Serve with cilantro garnish. Quinoa is higher in protein than any other grain, and I often use it in preference to others.

Variations: Try adding ½ cup of pistachios instead of beans. Quinoa and many of the other grains may also be served as a salad with onions, tomato, cucumber, celery, and any other salad combination. I keep frozen edamame on hand and find it easier to use in small portions than opening a can of garbanzos.

[VIII]

EGGS, CHEESE, TOFU, and NUTS

For pescetarians and vegetarians, eggs, cheese, tofu, and nuts are commonly consumed almost daily, for protein as well as to please the palate. It is wise to be aware of the source when buying eggs, since outbreaks of salmonella have occurred on chicken farms in some states in the U.S.

Nuts add flavor as well as texture to any food, and nuts are also available in delicious variety: pistachios, walnuts, almonds, peanuts, pecans, cashews, filberts, Brazil nuts, macadamia nuts, gingko nuts, and pine nuts.

For cheese there are more varieties than we can mention. Ten varieties are listed for the Middle East, eleven for Austria, twelve for Germany, thirty-eight for Greece, and an astonishing over one thousand for France! Obviously we will not mention or include recipes for this amazing abundance. Cheeses may be categorized as soft, medium, or hard. Common soft cheeses include brie, mozzarella, muenster, ricotta, and Roquefort.

Among the medium cheeses are for Colby and Monterey jack. Harder varieties include asiago, cheddar, gouda, gruyere, parmesan, provolone, Romano, and Swiss.

Tofu, the soy bean cake common in many if not most Asian recipes, is also generally classified as soft, medium, or firm. Sometimes "silk" is used to describe a soft tofu.

Here we include a sampling of recipes for these four sources of protein.

Mushroom Quiche

1 egg, beaten

2 large crimini or shiitake mushrooms

1 scallion or green onion, chopped

1 tablespoon olive oil or butter

⅓ cup grated cheddar cheese

½ cup half and half

1 tablespoon frozen peas

¼ teaspoon mustard

Salt and pepper to taste

Dash of red pepper

Beat the egg. Meanwhile, in a small frying pan sauté the onion and mushrooms in oil about 3 minutes. Add cheese, peas, seasonings and sautéed mushrooms to the beaten egg.

Crust:

⅓ cup all purpose flour

2 tablespoons butter

1 tablespoon ice water

Cut the butter into the flour, add water, and form a ball. Refrigerate 30 minutes. Then press it into a small tart pan and add the egg filling. Bake at 375 degrees 20 minutes. This is one of my favorite meals, For a large quiche multiply by 3 or 4 times.

Variation: Asparagus is an excellent addition, or also a substitute for mushrooms.

Shrimp Egg Foo Yung

1 large egg	2 tablespoons bean sprouts
1 scallion or green onion	2 shiitake mushrooms, sliced
1 teaspoon sesame oil	1 tablespoon olive oil
2 cooked, chopped shrimp	

Sauté scallions, mushrooms and sprouts in oil. Add beaten egg and shrimp, and cook, stirring, then cover and cook 3 minutes.

Sauce:

1 teaspoon ketchup

¼ teaspoon soy sauce

¼ teaspoon rice vinegar

1 teaspoon oyster sauce

½ teaspoon cornstarch

Mix all ingredients and simmer 2 minutes, stirring constantly. Serve over the egg.

Variation: Instead of oyster sauce, which many cooks do not keep in the larder, try dashi granules in water. Both these ingredients are available in Asian food stores.

Curried Egg

1 egg	1 tablespoon butter or ghee
2 teaspoons flour	¼ teaspoon cumin powder
¼ teaspoon coriander	¼ teaspoon turmeric
Salt and pepper to taste	1 tablespoon chopped onion

Boil the egg at least three minutes, until yolk is firm. In a frying pan sauté the onion in butter until translucent, then add the cumin, coriander and turmeric and cook an additional 30 seconds. Peel the egg and cut into quarters lengthwise. Serve over basmati rice. This is a simple preparation and is also appropriate for brunch, served with scones or breakfast pastry.

Variation: For a spicier version add a dash of cayenne pepper. Cilantro is also a good garnish for this preparation, as in many Indian recipes.

Cheese Soufflé

1 egg, white & yolk separated

1 tablespoon cream or half and half

Dash of cayenne pepper

2 teaspoons butter

2 tablespoons grated cheddar

Salt and pepper to taste

2 teaspoons flour

Melt butter over low heat and slowly blend in flour and cream. Cook briefly stirring continually until slightly thickened. Add seasoning and reduce heat and stir in the cheese. When cheese is melted add beaten egg yolk and cook for one minute. Cool these ingredients. Then stiffly beat egg white and fold lightly into the cheese mixture. Place soufflé in a small ungreased baking dish in a moderate oven, 350 degrees. After 10 minutes reduce the heat slightly and bake until the soufflé is firm, about a total of 30 minutes.

Variation: Since this preparation requires several steps you may prefer to double or triple the recipe. This is a good dish to serve with brunch.

Mushroom-Cheese Frittata

1 egg	2 teaspoons mozzarella
2 teaspoons chopped onion	2 crimini mushrooms
2 teaspoons chopped red bell pepper	1 roma tomato, chopped
Dash of thyme	Salt and pepper to taste
2 teaspoons oil or butter	

Sauté onion in oil or butter, adding red pepper first, then mushrooms 2 minutes later. Then add tomato and mozzarella and cook an additional minute. Lastly, add the beaten egg, salt and pepper.

Variation: This simple, versatile recipe may be varied in any way you choose—with the addition of chopped asparagus, zucchini, or arugula—for example. If you prefer a spicier version, add a dash of cayenne pepper or some chopped anchovies. Garnish with parsley or cilantro.

Egg and Cheese Tortilla

1 tablespoon. oil or butter	1 flour or corn tortilla
1 egg	2 tablespoons cheddar or pepper jack
1 teaspoon chopped mild green chili	1 tablespoon chopped tomato
1 tablespoon chopped onion or shallot	

Melt butter in a non-stick skillet and sauté onion. Beat egg in a small bowl and add the grated cheese, chili and tomato. Heat the tortilla in the warm skillet for about 1 minute or until lightly toasted. Then pour the egg-vegetable mixture over the tortilla and spread evenly. Flip the tortilla over so that the egg side is down and cook, pressing lightly with a spatula. When the egg is cooked, remove to a plate, egg side up, sprinkle with cheese, and roll up.

Variation: Serve with salsa, guacamole, or caper garnish. Try adding a dash of toasted, crushed fennel seeds with a few cooked pinto beans.

Cheese and Corn Fritters

½ cup flour

1 heaping tablespoon cornmeal

1 teaspoon baking powder

1 large tablespoon butter, melted

1 large tablespoon grated cheddar

½ cup corn kernels

2 teaspoons sugar

5 tablespoons buttermilk

1 tablespoon oil

1 egg, beaten

1 teaspoon saffron threads soaked in 2 tablespoons water

Salt to taste

Stir together flour, cornmeal, baking powder, sugar and salt. Combine egg, buttermilk and saffron. Fold in dry ingredients, then stir in melted butter, cheese and last, the corn. Heat vegetable oil in pan until very hot. Drop fritter mixture into oil by tablespoon and fry about 5 minutes or until golden brown. Watch cooking temperature closely Serve while warm. Garnish with parsley and chopped green onion.

Crepes

¼ cup sifted flour	1 egg, beaten
1 tablespoon powdered sugar	1 tablespoon sherry
Pinch of salt and pepper	2 teaspoons oil or butter
¼ cup milk or cream	¼ teaspoon grated lemon rind

Sift flour, sugar and salt together. Stir in cream. Add beaten egg, some of the wine, melted butter and grated lemon rind. Grease a pan and cook until light brown.

Sprinkle with powdered sugar and remaining wine. Roll and serve hot.

Variation: You may also add your favorite jam—strawberry, apricot, or your choice--to the crepe before rolling. This is another excellent brunch selection.

Goat Cheese-Vegetable Wrap

1 mushroom, sliced	2 teaspoons red bell pepper, chopped
1 tablespoon eggplant, cubed	1 green onion, chopped
1 tablespoon olive tapenade	1 teaspoon lemon juice
2 tablespoons goat cheese, crumbled	
1 corn or wheat tortilla	Salt and pepper to taste
2 teaspoons oil	Arugula leaves

Sauté mushroom, bell pepper, eggplant and onion in oil. Toss in a bowl with lemon juice, goat cheese, salt and pepper. Line tortilla with arugula leaves, then cover tortilla with cheese-vegetable mixture. Wrap tightly, tucking in the ends and serve.

Tofu with Rice Noodles

⅓ - ½ firm tofu cubes	1 green onion
1 teaspoon sesame oil	1 teaspoon olive oil
½ teaspoon chopped garlic	1 teaspoon grated ginger root
1 mushroom, sliced	1-2 tablespoons chopped bok choy
1 teaspoon soy sauce	Handful of dried noodles

Cook rice noodles in boiling water until soft, about 8 minutes. Meanwhile, sauté onion, ginger, and garlic in oil combination. Add mushroom and bok choy 3 minutes later. Lastly, add tofu cubes and soy sauce.

Variation: Try adding cut up asparagus spears, 1 tablespoon of sake, and/or a very thinly sliced fried egg and a dash of cayenne pepper. If you don't have bok choy, use Napa cabbage. Shrimp is also an excellent addition.

Nut Loaf

¼ cup chopped onion

1 cup grated carrot

2 eggs, beaten

⅓ cup chopped walnuts

Dash of basil and oregano

1 tablespoon chopped green pepper

⅓ cup sliced mushrooms

1 tablespoon butter

1 stalk celery, chopped

1 cup bread crumbs

Salt and pepper to taste

Sauté onion, pepper and mushrooms in butter. Combine all ingredients in a bowl and lastly stir in bread crumbs and beaten egg. Bake in a greased pan at 350 degrees until meat thermometer reads 160 degrees. Let stand 10 minutes before slicing. Serves 2.

Variation: Garnish with red bell pepper sauce.

Fried Tofu and Zucchini

½ cup cubed firm tofu

½ cup sliced zucchini

2 tablespoons sliced onion

1 teaspoon minced garlic

1 teaspoon minced ginger

1 teaspoon soy sauce

1 tablespoon rice wine or sherry

½ teaspoon cider vinegar

1 tablespoon cornstarch

1 teaspoon sugar

1 tablespoon water

1 tablespoon scallion or green onion

1 tablespoon sesame oil

Combine liquids in a cup, adding water to cornstarch separately. Heat onion in oil, fry 2 minutes. Add zucchini, pinch of salt, and fry 8 minutes. Add garlic and ginger and cook 2 more minutes. Add tofu and liquids with cornstarch. Stir. Garnish with scallion greens.

Variation: Other squash may be used with or instead of zucchini, for example, summer squash. Tofu is versatile and can be used with a variety of vegetables.

[IX]

BREADS AND MUFFINS

Breads made with yeast come in a variety, depending on the grain milled for the flour. Most yeast breads are made with white or whole wheat flour. For individuals with a wheat sensitivity or Celiac, many other acceptable flours are available in health food stores. These flours include amaranth, buckwheat, almond and other nut flours, chickpea flour, oat flour, potato flour, rice flour, soy flour, and teff. For individuals with a slight wheat sensitivity, spelt flour (from an ancient variety of wheat) is a good alternative to regular wheat flour. Some of these flours require a bit of guar gum. It has become customary for people to say "wheat bread," when they mean whole wheat bread, as if white bread were not also made from wheat.

Yeast breads require time to allow the dough to rise twice and are therefore time consuming. An easier way to cook yeasts bread is to use a bread machine, which does the kneading and rising automatically, saving the cook an hour and a half of preparation time. But if you enjoy the process of kneading and have the time, do it the old-fashioned way.

Breads and muffins made with vegetables and fruits are sweeter and do not require yeast. As a result, they take less preparation time, but of course they don't have the traditional bread flavor or aroma coming out of the oven. These are some of my favorite breads. Scones are popular for brunch and also do not require yeast.

In this chapter we include a basic yeast bread recipe which can be varied in any imaginable number of ways. Most recipes in this chapter are for non-yeast, sweet breads, muffins and scones.

Basic Yeast Bread

1 cup warm water (120 degrees F)	1 dry yeast tablet or grains
¼ cup sugar or honey	1 teaspoon salt
3 cup all-purpose flour	2 tablespoons butter or vegetable oil

Dissolve sugar, then yeast, in warm water in a large bowl. Mix in salt and oil. Add flour one cup at a time. Knead dough on lightly floured board for five minutes, then knead again until smooth. Place in a well oiled bowl and cover with a damp cloth. Allow to rise to double in bulk, about one hour. Pinch down and knead a few minutes. Shape into 2 loaves and put in oiled loaf pans. Allow to rise until dough is one inch above the pan. Preheat oven to 425 degrees and bake 10 minutes, then turn down the oven to 350 degrees and cook another 20 minutes. Makes one loaf.

Variation: Try adding a teaspoon of cumin and zest of one orange to the dough for a palatable bread. Many other herbs also create unique flavors. Try replacing honey with molasses and replacing 1/4 of the flour with cornmeal, for New England Anadama bread.

Zucchini Bread

1 ½ cup flour	½ teaspoon salt
½ teaspoon soda	1 ½ teaspoon cinnamon
¼ teaspoon baking powder	⅔ cup oil
1 ½ teaspoon vanilla	1 egg
1 ½ cup grated zucchini	½ cup chopped walnuts

Sift dry ingredients together. Beat the egg and add vanilla and grated zucchini.

Combine all ingredients, adding nuts last. Bake in a greased loaf pan at 350 degrees for one hour. Check at 40 minutes. Makes one loaf.

Variation: Many variations are possible by replacing zucchini with fruit, for example peaches, cranberries, strawberries, blueberries, or a combination of your favorite fruits.

Apricot Almond Bread

2 ¼ cup flour	1 cup dried apricots, cut up
1 cup rolled oats	1 cup almonds, chopped
1 cup turbinado sugar	1 egg, beaten
1 teaspoon salt	¾ cup orange juice
½ teaspoon baking powder	2 tablespoons orange zest
¼ teaspoon baking soda	2 tablespoons soft butter
2 cups warm water	2 tablespoons amaretto

Cream butter and sugar, then add the egg, orange zest, amaretto and orange juice. Mix dry ingredients, then add apricots and nuts. Combine all ingredients. Bake in greased pan at 350 degrees for one hour or until an inserted toothpick comes out clean.

Variation: Try using a bit of almond flour with the regular flour. Actually, many other fruits may be used in place of apricots—raspberries, strawberries, cranberries, etc., but apricots and almonds are a great pairing.

Banana Bread

2 cups flour

1 teaspoon salt

1 cup sugar

4 very ripe bananas

1 teaspoon baking soda

½ cup butter

2 eggs, beaten

In a large bowl cream butter and sugar. Beat in eggs one at a time and stir until smooth. Sift dry ingredients together in a smaller bowl. Mash the bananas into a puree. Add dry ingredients and butter mixture alternating with banana, starting and ending with the flour. Add more flour if the batter is too runny. Pour into a greased 8 x 8" loaf pan. Bake one hour in a preheated oven at 350 degrees. Check at 20 minutes.

Variation: Try adding a handful of chopped walnuts or almonds.

Oatmeal Spelt Muffins

½ cup quick oats

⅔ cup spelt flour

4 teaspoons salt

½ cup yogurt

¼ cup brown sugar

¼ cup walnuts or almonds, chopped

¼ cup oil or butter

1 teaspoon baking powder

¼ teaspoon baking soda

1 egg, beaten

⅓ cup dried cranberries

Add oats to yogurt and soak 30 minutes. Sift flour with dry ingredients, then add oats. Add sugar, oil and egg to oat mixture. Combine all ingredients, adding cranberries and nuts last. Bake in greased muffin tins at 450 degrees or until brown, about 20 minutes.

Variation: Raisins or currants may be substituted for cranberries.

Scotch Scones

1 ½ cup flour	1 ½ cup old fashioned oats
¼ cup sugar	½ teaspoon salt
1 teaspoon baking powder	1 teaspoon cream of tartar
⅓ cup currants or cranberries	⅔ cup butter
⅓ cup milk	1 egg

Mix dry ingredients together. Cream butter and sugar together. Beat the egg and combine all ingredients, adding the fruit last. Bake in a 400 degree oven in a large greased pan until lightly brown on top, about 20 minutes. Test with a toothpick.

Variation: A fourth of a cup of nuts such as walnuts or almonds may also be added I often use a pie pan for this recipe

Ginger Orange Scones

1 ¼ cup cake flour, sifted	3 tablespoons granulated sugar
½ teaspoon baking powder	Pinch of salt
Zest of 1 orange	⅓ cup chopped candied ginger
¾ stick of chilled butter	¼ cup + 2 tablespoons heavy cream
½ teaspoon vanilla	turbinado sugar to top

In a food processor, pulse flour, sugar, baking powder and salt. Add orange zest, ginger, and butter cut into small pieces and pulse until the mixture has the consistency of cornmeal. Transfer to a bowl and add cream and vanilla. Gather dough together, adding a teaspoon of cream if too dry. On a floured surface, gently knead and press together to form a disk about ¾ inch thick. Sprinkle lightly with turbinado sugar. Cut into 4 wedges and place on an ungreased baking sheet. Bake in a preheated oven at 350 degrees until the tops are lightly golden, about 12 minutes. This recipe is one of my favorites. Be sure that the butter is chilled, not frozen, and cut up, and also to use cake flour.

Variation: Lemon juice and zest may be substituted for orange zest. Use the juice of one lemon.

L i g h t Gingerbread

2 eggs	½ cup honey
½ cup sugar	½ cup molasses
1 cup canola oil	1 cup brewed spice tea
2 ½ cup flour	½ teaspoon ginger
½ teaspoon baking soda	½ teaspoon cinnamon
½ teaspoon salt	

Sift together dry ingredients. Beat eggs, add oil, honey and molasses.

Combine liquids with flour and mix thoroughly. In an 8 x 8" pan, bake in a preheated oven, 350 degrees for about 20 minutes. Serve warm or at room temperature with whipped cream. Add 1 tablespoon powdered sugar and ½ teaspoon five spice powder to the cream before whipping. This recipe is not as overpowering as some gingerbread.

Cornbread

1 cup flour	1 teaspoon salt
1 cup cornmeal	3 teaspoons baking powder
½ cup sugar	1 egg
1 cup buttermilk	1 teaspoon baking soda
⅓ cup vegetable oil	

Preheat oven to 400 degrees. Grease an 8 x 8 inch pan. Combine dry ingredients, add milk, egg and oil and stir well. Bake 20 to 25 minutes or until an inserted toothpick comes out clean.

Variation: Add a fourth of a cup of grated mozzarella and/or a dash of red pepper flakes. Or try adding chopped scallions or green onions.

Lemon Poppy Seed Bread

1 ½ cup flour	¾ cup sugar
½ cup milk	1 egg, beaten
1 tablespoon lemon juice	1 tablespoon lemon zest
1 teaspoon baking powder	½ teaspoon salt
½ cup softened butter	1 tablespoon poppy seeds
½ teaspoon vanilla	½ teaspoon lemon extract
1 ½ tablespoon melted butter	

Glaze: 3 tablespoons sugar, 1 tablespoon lemon juice, 1 ½ tablespoon melted butter, mixed.

Combine dry ingredients with softened butter and pulse. Add beaten egg, vanilla, lemon extract, milk and melted butter and mix thoroughly. Pour into greased 8 x 8" pan and bake 35 minutes in preheated 350 degree oven. Cool in the pan 10 minutes, remove from the pan and pour glaze over bread. This sweet bread has a cake-like consistency and may be served as dessert, warm or at room temperature with whipped cream of lemon sauce.

Date Nut Bread

¾ cup Sherry	1 teaspoon baking soda
1 cup pitted dates, cut up	¼ cup shortening
1 cup sugar	2 eggs, beaten
1 teaspoon vanilla	2 cups sifted flour
1 teaspoon baking powder	½ teaspoon salt
½ cup walnuts, chopped	

Heat sherry to just short of boiling. Sprinkle soda over dates in a bowl.

Pour sherry over the dates and cool. Cream shortening and sugar together. Add cooled sherry mixture, beaten eggs and vanilla. Mix well. Add flour with baking powder and salt to creamed mixture, stirring until blended. Add nuts. Bake 40 minutes in greased 8 x 8" pan in preheated oven, 350 degrees. Check at 30 minutes. This is a dessert bread.

Variation: Use water instead of Sherry, if you prefer. Pecans are also good with this recipe. Or replace Sherry with hot coffee for an unusual treat.

Pumpkin Bread

⅓ cup vegetable shortening	¾ cup sugar
2 eggs, beaten	1 cup pumpkin puree
⅓ cup buttermilk	1 tablespoon bourbon
1 ¾ cup flour	¼ teaspoon baking powder
1 teaspoon baking soda	1 teaspoon salt
1 ½ teaspoon cinnamon	½ teaspoon grated nutmeg
½ cup pecans or walnuts	

Preheat oven to 350 degrees and grease 8 x 8" pan. With an electric mixer cream shortening and sugar, then beat in eggs one at a time until fluffy. Beat in pumpkin puree, buttermilk and bourbon until smooth. Separately sift dry ingredients. Add dry ingredients to pumpkin mixture a little at a time until combined. Fold in nuts. Bake for one hour until toothpick comes out clean. Cool in pans five minutes, invert onto racks, and cool.

Variation: Serve with whipped cream garnished with grated nutmeg if desired.

Harvest Bread

1 cup flour	1 teaspoon baking powder
Pinch of salt	1 teaspoon cinnamon
⅔ cup sugar	¾ cup finely shredded carrot
½ cup flake coconut	1 tart apple, peeled, cored, shredded
⅓ cup raisins	½ cup canola oil
1 egg. slightly beaten	½ teaspoon vanilla extract
⅓ cup chopped pecans	

Combine flour, baking powder, salt and cinnamon. Stir in sugar, apples, carrot, coconut, raisins and pecans. In a well in the center combine eggs, oil and vanilla and stir into dry ingredients. Do not overmix. Bake at 350 degrees in an 8 x8" greased loaf pan or 3 mini pans, 30 minutes for small pans, longer for loaf pans. Turn out of pans and cool before slicing. This fruitcake-like recipe can also be used for muffins. Preparation is a bit time-consuming.

Pear Bread

2 cups pears, peeled and cut up	½ cup butter
1 cup sugar	½ teaspoon baking soda
2 eggs	1 teaspoon baking powder
2 cups flour	1 teaspoon vanilla
½ teaspoon salt	⅛ teaspoon grated nutmeg
¼ cup yogurt or buttermilk	

Preheat oven to 350 degrees and grease a loaf pan. Cream butter and sugar, then add eggs singly, beating each. Combine dry ingredients and add alternately with milk and vanilla. Bake one hour, checking at 40 minutes with a toothpick.

Variation: Try adding 2 teaspoons of brandy.

[X]

DESSERTS

There are literally limitless possibilities for desserts. Selection is a matter of individual taste and tolerance for sugar and fats. Since many Americans suffer from obesity and attendant diseases, caution is advisable. I personally enjoy rich desserts, and fortunately not everyone suffers from a weight problem.

Some desserts can be as simple as fruit in season, with or without the addition of cream or a liqueur. Others are more complex, involving flours with other ingredients and requiring baking. Since one purpose of this book is to encourage reluctant cooks, we do not include here many complicated recipes for cakes. An elegant dessert can be prepared, for example, using mini graham cracker crusts, adding your favorite seasonal fruit, a bit of sugar and flour, and a dollop of French crème fraiche. Bake these for eight or ten minutes and you have a dessert fit for a king, or your guests. I admit to a weakness for cookies and therefore include a few recipes for these crumbly desserts. Desserts are the perfect coda to a satisfying meal.

Peanut Butter Cookies

½ cup shortening

½ cup peanut butter (chunky)

½ cup brown sugar

½ cup white sugar

1 egg

1 cup flour

1 teaspoon soda

¼ teaspoon salt

½ teaspoon vanilla extract

Cream shortening and peanut butter together and add sugar. Add beaten egg and vanilla. Sift flour, soda and salt together and add to egg mixture. Form dough into balls about one inch in diameter and flatten with a fork, crosswise. Bake in 375 degree oven on a greased cookie sheet 12 to 15 minutes or until light brown. Yield: 40 two-inch cookies.

This old time recipe is near the top of my list of favorites.

Scotch Shortbread

⅔ cup butter

½ cup sugar

1 ½ cup flour

½ teaspoon salt

Cream butter and sugar together, then add sifted flour and salt. Roll out to half an inch thick, cut into shapes and place on greased cookie tin. Bake at 300 degrees about 25 minutes. You can sprinkle the cut out cookies with a bit of turbinado sugar before baking and or course these standard cookies can be decorated with colored frosting for special occasions. A simple frosting can be made with powdered sugar, softened butter, and a flavoring such as vanilla, orange zest and a bit of juice, or chocolate bits or melted chocolate.

Oatmeal Cookies

1 ½ cup old fashioned oats	½ cup flour
⅓ cup + 3 tablespoons butter	⅔ cup turbinado sugar
½ teaspoon vanilla	1 egg
½ teaspoon baking soda	¼ teaspoon salt
½ teaspoon cinnamon	½ cup raisins

Cream butter and sugar together, add egg and vanilla and beat. Add combined flour, cinnamon, baking soda and salt. Mix well. Add oats and raisins. Drop dough in marble sized balls onto an ungreased cookie sheet and bake in 350 degree oven 12 to 15 minutes.

Variation: Add cranberries in place of raisins. Or replace part of fruit with bittersweet chocolate chips or flaked coconut. This is another old favorite.

Date Nut Bars

1 ½ cup flour	1 teaspoon baking powder
½ teaspoon salt	3 eggs
1 cup dark corn syrup	½ cup oil
½ teaspoon vanilla	1 cup chopped dates
½ cup chopped nuts	

Stir together flour, baking powder and salt. In a separate bowl beat eggs with a mixer, then add corn syrup, oil, vanilla, dates and nuts. Beat until well mixed. Stir in dry ingredients. Bake in a greased 8 x 8" pan in a 350 degree oven until tester comes out clean, about 45 minutes. Use pecans or walnuts, possibly almonds.

Variation: If desired glaze with powdered sugar, cream and lemon juice.

Spice Bars

½ cup butter

¾ cup turbinado sugar

1 large egg

⅓ cup milk

½ teaspoon baking soda

Pinch of salt

1 cup flour

½ teaspoon nutmeg

½ teaspoon cinnamon

¾ cup raisins

⅓ cup chopped pecans or walnuts

Cream butter and sugar together. Add beaten egg and milk. Blend dry ingredients and add to butter-sugar mixture. Add raisins and nuts last. Bake in a greased 8 x 8" pan at 375 degrees for 10 to 12 minutes. Frost with powdered sugar, cream and lemon juice with a bit of lemon zest.

Variation: Replace raisins with cranberries or chopped dried apricots.

Mini Pumpkin Cheesecakes

⅓ cup soft cream cheese   ¼ cup pumpkin puree

2 tablespoons turbinado sugar   1 tablespoon flour

½ teaspoon grated ginger root   1 tablespoon buttermilk

Dash of nutmeg   ⅛ teaspoon cinnamon

Dash of allspice

Crust: Use 2 or 3 mini graham cracker crusts, or crush gingersnaps, mix with melted butter and press into small tart pans. Fill crusts with pumpkin puree and bake 12-15 minutes at 350 degrees. Serve with a dollop of crème fraiche and sprinkle with grated nutmeg. If you use ginger snaps, you need to use a food processor to ensure that they are finely crushed.

Variation: When making a simple pumpkin pie, add 2 teaspoons of orange zest or a teaspoon of brandy or rum. You can also use commercially available mini graham cracker crusts.

Rum Fruit Balls

38 graham cracker squares crushed   ½ cup powdered sugar

¼ cup light corn syrup   ¼ cup rum

1 cup raisins   ½ cup candied cherries, chopped

⅓ cup semi-sweet chocolate chips

Mix all ingredients and shape into one inch balls. Let sit on waxed paper for two or three hours. No cooking is necessary.

Graham Cracker Log

30 graham crackers

10 maraschino cherries

10 marshmallows, cut up

1 small can pineapple

1 cup walnuts or almonds, chopped

½ cup heavy cream

Crush graham crackers, drain pineapple and add it, cherries and nuts to the crackers. Add cream, mix well and form into a log. If necessary, add a bit more cream. Cover with foil and place in freezer. Remove from freezer half an hour before serving. Slice and serve with whipped cream or crème fraiche. This unique dessert also requires no cooking and was one of my mother's favorites to serve to guests.

Polish Tea Cakes

½ cup butter   1 cup flour

½ cup sugar   ½ teaspoon salt

1 egg yolk, beaten   ½ teaspoon vanilla

Cream butter and sugar until fluffy. Add egg yolk and vanilla and mix. Add sifted flour with salt. Roll dough into small balls, dip in unbeaten egg white and roll in chopped nuts. Place on cookie sheet and bake at 350 degrees 10 minutes. Remove and with a thimble press down in center and bake 5 more minutes. Remove and while warm fill indentation with your favorite preserves. A Polish friend made these for holidays.

Chocolate Brownies

½ cup butter

2 eggs

½ cup flour

1 teaspoon vanilla

Confectioners sugar

1 teaspoon rum or amaretto

2 square unsweetened chocolate

¾ cup turbinado sugar

1 teaspoon baking powder

½ cup semisweet chocolate chips

⅓ cup almonds or pecans, chopped

Dash of cinnamon.

Melt butter and chocolate in microwave. Cool slightly. In a large bowl beat eggs, gradually ad sugar and beat. Combine flour and baking powder, add to egg mixture. Stir in chocolate, vanilla and chips. Bake on high 4 minutes. Remove to rack, cool 10 minutes and dust with confectioners sugar.

Variation: Of course you can omit the rum and cinnamon for more conventional brownies. Everyone has a favorite brownie recipe, but this distinctive one is mine. It verges on fudge.

Lemon Bars

6-8 tablespoon butter

1 ¼ cup flour

¼ cup confectioners sugar

This is the crust: Combine all together and pulse in a processor. Press into a greased pan and bake in a preheated 350 degree oven about 20 minutes, till light golden.

Topping:

2 eggs	1 cup + 1 tablespoon sugar
Juice of 3 lemons	1 tablespoon lemon zest
1 tablespoon flour	Pinch of salt

In a bowl beat eggs and add other ingredients. Pour onto crust and bake at 350 degrees about 5 minutes. Cool on a rack and dust with confectioners sugar.

This recipe works at high altitude. Don't forget to use high altitude flour if above 4,000 feet.

Strawberry Rhubarb Crisp

2 cups strawberries, cut up   2 cups rhubarb cut up

½ cup sugar   ½ cup oats

½ teaspoon cinnamon   ½ cup flour

¼ teaspoon salt   Dash of nutmeg and allspice

5 tablespoons melted butter   ¼ cup brown sugar

Combine fruit with a bit of sugar and cinnamon in 8 x 8" pan. Mix all other ingredients in a bowl and sprinkle over the fruit evenly. Bake 35 minutes in a preheated 400 degree oven till the top is browned and the fruit bubbles. Serve warm or at room temperature with vanilla ice cream or French crème fraiche.

Indian Rice Pudding (Kheer)

½ cup short grain rice

8 cups whole milk

4 green cardamom pods

¾ cup sugar

Wash the rice. Tap the cardamom pods until they slightly open. Pour the milk and cardamom into a large, heavy saucepan and bring milk to a boil, then reduce the heat and add the rice, simmering about 25 minutes while stirring constantly with a wooden spoon. Then reduce the heat further to a low boil for another 10 minutes. When it becomes slightly thick remove from the heat and extract the cardamom pods. Stir in sugar and allow to cool.

Variation: Sliced almonds and golden raisins are a good addition to the kheer. In some parts of India rose water is added as well. To make a simpler version, just add coconut milk to the other rice and seasonings. With raisins sugar is unnecessary.

Strawberry Pie

1 quart berries	3 tablespoons cornstarch
3-4 oz. cream cheese	1 tablespoon lemon juice
¼ cup sugar	Whipped cream

Bake and cool a 9" pie shell. Put softened cream cheese across the bottom. Place choicest berries firmly into cheese, tips up. Mash the other berries, strain, and add water to make 1 ½ cup liquid. Mix sugar and cornstarch in a pan. Add berries and lemon juice. Cook, stirring constantly until it thickens clear, 5-6 minutes. Add red color if desired.

Cool and pour into shell. Cool 3 hours before serving. Decorate with whipped cream or French crème fraiche.

Variation: Consider using a graham cracker crust for this recipe.

Pecan Pie

3 eggs, beaten

1 teaspoon vanilla

1 cup pecans

Dash of cinnamon

1 cup pecans, whole or pieces

½ cup brown sugar

1 cup dark Karo syrup

4 tablespoons melted butter

2 teaspoons bourbon or brandy

Beat eggs and add other ingredients. Put in an unbaked pie shell and bake 1 hour at 350 degrees. Check at 40 minutes to avoid burning the crust.

Pineapple Macadamia Fruitcake

2 ½ cup candied pineapple chunks

1 cup salted macadamia nuts

½ cup flaked coconut

2 tablespoons flour

¾ cup sugar

⅓ cup + 2 tablespoons butter

3 xeggs

1 tablespoon milk

1 tablespoon pineapple extract

½ teaspoon vanilla

1 cup flour

¼ cup rum

Preheat oven to 300 degrees. Grease 2 loaf pans or 4 mini loaf pans.

Line with wax paper and grease the paper. Toss 2 cups pineapple with nuts and coconut, coat with 2 Tbsp flour, set aside.

In a large bowl at medium speed beat sugar and butter till fluffy. Add eggs, singly, beating after each. Beat in milk, flavoring, and at low speed beat in flour.

Stir in fruit and nuts, then spoon batter into pans and top with pineapple, pressing slightly. Bake 1 ¼ hours, cool on wire racks 15 minutes, remove wax paper and wrap in foil. Store in fridge up to a month, in freezer up to 3 months. Fruitcakes take time.

Lacy Ginger Cookies

½ cup molasses

⅔ cup sugar

1 tablespoon confectioners sugar

1 stick unsalted butter

1 sparse cup flour

Heat the oven to 300 degrees and place foil over a cookie sheet. Melt the butter and gradually add molasses, sugar and flour. Take off the heat and drop by teaspoonfuls. Leaving 1 ½" spaces. Bake 10 minutes. Let cool slightly. Roll around a wooden spoon if you can.

Decadent Chocolate Mousse

6 oz. semisweet chocolate pieces   2 tablespoons sugar

¾ cup milk   1 egg

1 teaspoon vanilla   ¼ teaspoon salt

Place all ingredients except milk in a blender. Heat milk to just below boiling. Pour milk into blender and blend 1 minute, covered. Pour into a bowl or serving dish and chill. Serve with whipped cream or ice cream. Guests always request the recipe.

Apricot Cloud

6 oz. dried apricots	2 cups boiling water
½ cup + 2 tablespoons sugar	1 envelope unflavored gelatin
1 cup yogurt	½ teaspoon vanilla
2 teaspoons lemon juice	Kiwi slices for garnish

Soften gelatin in 14 cup cold water. Boil apricots in non-metallic saucepan covered. Let stand 2 hours, then simmer till apricots are tender but not mushy, 20 minutes. Stir in ½ cup sugar. Puree hot apricots with juice in a blender, add softened gelatin and mix. Put in a bowl, cover and refrigerate until set. In a bowl beat yogurt with a fork, mix into apricots with vanilla, then chill. Beat egg whites, add lemon juice and bet till peaks form. Beat in sugar 1 Tbsp at a time. Fold into apricot mixture. Spoon into a serving bowl and garnish with apricot pieces and kiwi slices.

Easy Key Lime Pie

1 graham cracker crust

1 can Eagle condensed milk

½ cup fresh lime juice (or key lime juice)

Warm crust 5 minutes in 350 degree oven, then cool the crust. Squeeze lime juice and combine with condensed milk in a bowl. Spread on the cooled crust. Place in freezer until half an hour before serving. Again, no cooking is required for this simple recipe which always wins praise from guests.

USEFUL INGREDIENTS FOR THE LARDER

This list may contain some ingredients unfamiliar to you. If so, start with those that are commonly used in most cooking. We begin with the essentials: salt and pepper.

Salt:
- Kosher salt
- Ordinary table salt
- Sea salt
- Hawaiian red salt

Pepper:
- Powdered:
  - Black
  - White
  - Red
- Whole:
  - Anaheim
  - Jalapeno
  - Poblano
  - Red Chili

Flours:
- All-purpose
- Cake flour
- High altitude flour
  (above 3,000 feet)
- Spelt flour
- Rice flour
- Potato flour
- Amaranth flour

Grains:
- Amaranth
- Cous cous
- Millet
- Quinoa

Rice varieties:
- Basmati, brown and white
- Black rice
- Jasmine rice
- Red rice
- Short grain white
- Long grain white
- Wild rice
  (though not strictly rice)

Herbs:
- Basil
- Cilantro
- Dill
- Fennel
- Lemongrass
- Marjoram
- Oregano
- Parsley
- Sage
- Sorrel
- Tarragon
- Thyme

Oils:
- Canola
- Coconut
- Extra Virgin Olive
- Macadamia Nut
- Peanut

Seasoning Sauces:
    Fish sauce
    Hoisin sauce
    Hot sauce
    Shoyu (soy sauce)

Spices:
    Asafoetida
    Cardamom
    Coriander
    Cumin
    Curry powder
    Old Bay seasoning (for fish)
    Red pepper
    Turmeric

Dried Seaweeds for Japanese Dishes:
    Hijiki
    Katsuo
    Kombu
    Nori
    Wakame

Vinegars:
    Balsamic
    Champagne
    Cider
    Pear
    Raspberry
    Red and White wine
    Sherry

Others:
    Edamame, frozen
    Miso paste